THE FOUR CARDINAL VIRTUES

The Four Cardinal Virtues

PRUDENCE

JUSTICE

FORTITUDE

TEMPERANCE

JOSEF PIEPER

Edition with Notes

UNIVERSITY OF NOTRE DAME PRESS

First paperback edition 1966 by
University of Notre Dame Press, Notre Dame, Indiana
Published by arrangement with Harcourt, Brace & World, Inc.

Library of Congress Catalog Card Number: 65-14713

The studies united here in one volume were published separately in this sequence:

Fortitude and *Temperance*	1954
Justice	1955
Prudence	1959

First published in Germany under the titles, *Vom Sinn der Tapferkeit, Zucht und Mass, Über die Gerechtigkeit, Traktat über die Klugheit,* by Kösel-Verlag. The present edition was edited by the author and slightly cut to avoid repetitions; notes and source references have been deleted. All quotations in the text are taken from works of Thomas Aquinas, unless the author is otherwise identified.

Prudence is a translation of *Traktat über die Klugheit,* and was translated by Richard and Clara Winston.
Justice is a translation of *Über die Gerechtigkeit,* and was translated by Lawrence E. Lynch.
Fortitude is a translation of *Vom Sinn der Tapferkeit,* and was translated by Daniel F. Coogan.
Temperance is a translation of *Zucht und Mass,* and was translated by Daniel F. Coogan.

Contents

CONTENTS

TEMPERANCE

THE FOUR CARDINAL VIRTUES

Preface

WHEN AGATHON in Plato's *Symposium* takes his turn at making a speech in praise of Love, he organizes his ideas around the four cardinal virtues: prudence, justice, fortitude, and temperance. An avant-garde intellectual who, incidentally, is the host at that famous banquet, Agathon offers no special reasons for this approach. That is, the contemporaries of Socrates already took for granted these traditional categories sprung from the earliest speculative thinking. They took for granted not only the idea of virtue, which signifies human rightness, but also the attempt to define it in that fourfold spectrum. This particular intellectual framework, the formula which is called the "doctrine of virtue," was one of the great discoveries in the history of man's self-understanding, and it has continued to be part and parcel of the European mind. It has become a basic component of the European consciousness, as the result of centuries of persistent intellectual endeavor by all the creative elements of the emerging West, both the Greeks (Plato, Aristotle) and the Romans (Cicero, Seneca), both Judaism (Philo) and Christianity (Clement of Alexandria, St. Augustine).

It is true that the classic origins of the doctrine of virtue later made Christian critics suspicious of it. They warily regarded it as too philosophical and not Scriptural enough. Thus, they preferred to talk about commandments and duties rather than about virtues. To define the obligations of man is certainly a legitimate, even estimable, and no doubt necessary undertaking. With a doctrine of commandments or duties, however, there is always the danger of arbitrarily drawing up a list of requirements and losing sight of the human person who "ought" to do this or that. The doctrine of virtue, on the other hand, has things to say about this human person; it speaks both of the kind of being which is his when he enters the world, as a consequence of his createdness, and the kind of being he ought to strive toward and attain to—by being prudent, just, brave, and temperate. The doctrine of virtue, that is, is one form of the doctrine of obligation; but one by nature free of regimentation and restriction. On the contrary, its aim is to clear a trail, to open a way.

But this is not the place to launch a disputation on the various possible modes of ethical statement. Rather, what I wish to do is to describe just one of those modes, and to reveal, as far as possible, its full reach: that team of four, the basic virtues, which, as a fine classical phrase put it, can enable man to attain the furthest potentialities of his nature.

In this realm, originality of thought and diction is of small importance—should, in fact, be distrusted. It can hardly be expected that there will be entirely new insights on such a subject. We may well turn to the "wisdom of the ancients" in our human quest to understand reality, for that wisdom contains a truly inexhaustible contemporaneity. The intention of this book is to reveal some of that contemporaneity.

Some readers may wonder why, in my effort to revive a classical heritage, I so often cite a certain medieval writer, Thomas Aquinas. I do so not from a more or less accidental historical interest, but because I believe that the testimony of the "universal teacher" of a still undivided Western Christianity has a special value. This lies not so much in his personal genius as in the truly creative selflessness with which he expressed the vast, contrapuntal range of possible statements about the cosmos—even as he recognized and called upon his readers to go beyond the limitations of his own vision. Marked though this thought is by an altogether extraordinary grasp and the most disciplined, dynamic, and penetrating independent thinking, there yet speaks through it less the individual writer, Thomas Aquinas, than the voice of the great tradition of human wisdom itself.

The interpreter, in these latter days, invokes this tradition in the hope of seeming less ridiculous as he boldly drafts a moral standard for humanity which he, in his own daily life, is utterly unable to meet.

PRUDENCE

---

*If thy eye is single, the whole
of thy body will be lit up.*
MATTHEW 6, 22

1. The First of the Cardinal Virtues

NO DICTUM in traditional Christian doctrine strikes such a note of strangeness to the ears of contemporaries, even contemporary Christians, as this one: that the virtue of prudence is the mold and "mother"[1] of all the other cardinal virtues, of justice, fortitude, and temperance. In other words, none but the prudent man can be just, brave, and temperate, and the good man is good in so far as he is prudent.

Our uneasiness and alienation would be only the greater if we were to take the proposition as seriously as it is meant. But we have grown accustomed to disregarding such hierarchic rankings among spiritual and ethical qualities. This is especially true for the "virtues." We assume that they are allegories, and that there is really no need to assign them an order of rank. We tend to think that it does not matter at all which of the four cardinal virtues may have drawn first prize in the lottery arranged by "scholastic" theologians.

Yet the fact is that nothing less than the whole ordered structure of the Occidental Christian view of man rests upon the pre-eminence of prudence over the other virtues. The structural framework of Occidental Christian metaphysics as a whole stands revealed, perhaps more plainly than in any other single ethical dictum, in the proposition that prudence is the foremost of the virtues. That structure is built thus: that Being precedes Truth, and that Truth precedes the Good.[2] Indeed, the living fire at the heart of the dictum is the central mystery of Christian theology: that the Father begets the Eternal Word, and that the Holy Spirit proceeds out of the Father and the Word.

Since this is so, there is a larger significance in the fact that people today can respond to this assertion of the pre-eminence of prudence only with incomprehension and uneasiness. That they feel it as strange may well reveal a deeper-seated and more total estrangement. It may mean that they no longer feel the binding force of the Christian Occidental view of man. It may denote the beginning of an incomprehension of the fundamentals of Christian teaching in regard to the nature of reality.

To the contemporary mind, prudence seems less a prerequisite to goodness than an evasion of it. The statement that it is prudence which makes an action good strikes us as well-nigh ridiculous. Should we hear it said, we tend to misunderstand the phrase, and take it as a tribute to undisguised utilitarianism. For we think of prudence as far more akin to the idea of mere utility, the *bonum utile*, than to the ideal of nobility, the *bonum honestum*. In colloquial use, prudence always carries the connotation of timorous, small-minded self-preservation, of a rather selfish concern about oneself. Neither of these traits is compatible with nobility; both are unworthy of the noble man.

It is therefore difficult for us to understand that the second cardinal virtue, justice, and all that is included in the word, can be said to derive from prudence. Certainly the common mind regards prudence and fortitude as virtually contradictory ideas. A "prudent" man is thought to be one who avoids the embarrassing situation of having to be brave. The "prudent" man is the "clever tactician" who contrives to escape personal commitment. Those who shun danger are wont to account for their attitude by appealing to the necessity for "prudence."

To the modern way of thinking, there seems to be a more obvious connection between prudence and the fourth cardinal virtue, that of temperance. But here too we will discover, if we dig deeper, that both these virtues are being beheld in quite a different light from the original great conception of them. For temperance, the disciplining of the instinctive craving for pleasure, was never meant to be exercised to induce a quietistic, philistine dullness. Yet this is what is implied in common phrases about "prudent moderation." That implication comes to the surface when people sneer at the noble daring of a celibate life, or the rigors of real fasting. They will speak scornfully of such practices as "imprudent exaggerations." In similar wise, they will condemn the forthright wrath of fortitude as aggressiveness.

To the contemporary mind, then, the concept of the good rather excludes than includes prudence. Modern man cannot conceive of a good act which might not be imprudent, nor of a bad act which might not be prudent. He will often call lies and cowardice prudent, truthfulness and courageous sacrifice imprudent.

Classical Christian ethics, on the contrary, maintains that man can be prudent and good only simultaneously; that prudence is part and parcel of the definition of goodness;[3] that there is no sort of justice and fortitude which runs counter to the virtue of prudence; and that the unjust man has been imprudent before and is imprudent at the moment he is unjust. *Omnis virtus moralis debet esse prudens*— All virtue is necessarily prudent.[4]

The general ethical attitudes of our era, as revealed in the conventions of everyday language, are shared by systematic moral theology—it is difficult to say which takes the lead, which is the follower. Perhaps both express a deeper process of spiritual change. At any rate, there is no doubt about the result: modern religious teachings have little or nothing to say about the place of prudence in life or in the hierarchy of virtues. Even the modern moral theologian who claims, or aspires, to be a follower of classical theology, displays this same uneasiness about prudence. One of the foremost contemporary theologians actually suggests that latter-day moral theologians have practiced a kind of suppression of the tract on prudence (*quasi-suppression du traité de la prudence*).[5] When an occasional contemporary treatise on moral theology does attempt to deal resolutely with Thomas Aquinas's doctrine of the virtues, the author, significantly enough, must spend much labor on a polemic justifying this "regression."[6]

Classical theology has been forced to resort to an immense variety of concepts and images in order to systematize the place of prudence and define its meaning with some degree of clarity. The very laboriousness of the definitions indicates that the classical theologians were here dealing with an essential problem of meaning and hierarchy, that the ordering of the virtues was not accidental.

Prudence is the *cause* of the other virtues' being virtues at all.[7] For example, there may be a kind of instinctive governance of instinctual cravings; but only prudence transforms this instinctive governance into the "virtue" of temperance.[8] Virtue is a "perfected ability" of man as a spiritual person; and justice, fortitude, and temperance, as "abilities" of the whole man, achieve their "perfection" only when they are founded upon prudence, that is to say upon the perfected ability to make right decisions. Only by means of this perfected ability to make good choices are instinctive inclinations toward goodness exalted into the spiritual core of man's decisions, from which truly human acts arise. Prudence is needed if man is to carry through his impulses and instincts for right acting, if he is to purify his naturally good predispositions and make them into real virtue, that is, into the truly human mode of "perfected ability." [9]

Prudence is the *"measure"* of justice, of fortitude, of temperance.[10]This means simply the following: as in the creative cognition of God all created things are pre-imaged and pre-formed; as, therefore, the immanent essences of all reality dwell in God as "ideas," as "preceding images" (to use the term of Meister Eckhart); and as man's perception of reality is a receptive transcript of the objective world of being; and as the artist's works are transcripts of a living prototype already within his creative cognition—so the decree of prudence is the prototype and the pre-existing form of which all ethically good action is the transcript. The precept of prudence is the "permanently exterior prototype"[11] by which the good deed is what it is; a good action becomes just, brave, temperate only as the consequence of the prototypal decree of prudence. Creation is what it is by its correspondence with the "standard" of God's creative knowledge; human cognition is true by its correspondence with the "standard" of objective reality. The work of art is true and real by its correspondence with the pattern of its prototype in the mind of the artist. In similar fashion, the free activity of man is good by its correspondence with the pattern of prudence. What is prudent and what is good are substantially one and the same; they differ only in their place in the logical succession of realization. For whatever is good must first have been prudent.[12]

Prudence *"informs"* the other virtues; it confers upon them the form of their inner essence. This dictum expresses the same idea in different manner. The "immanent essential form" of goodness, however, is in its very essence formed after that prototype, patterned after that pre-form. And so prudence imprints the inward seal of goodness upon all free activity of

7

man. Ethical virtue is the print and seal placed by prudence upon volition and action.[13] Prudence works in all the virtues;[14] and all virtue participates in prudence.[15]

All Ten Commandments of God pertain to the *executio prudentiae*,[16] the realization in practice of prudence. Here is a statement that has become virtually incomprehensible to people of today. And every sin is opposed to prudence. Injustice, cowardice, intemperance are in direct opposition to the virtues of justice, fortitude, and temperance; ultimately, however, through all these virtues, they run counter to prudence.[17] Everyone who sins is imprudent.[18]

Thus prudence is cause, root, mother, measure, precept, guide, and prototype of all ethical virtues; it acts in all of them, perfecting them to their true nature; all participate in it, and by virtue of this participation they are virtues.

The intrinsic goodness of man—and that is the same as saying his true humanness—consists in this, that "reason perfected in the cognition of truth" shall inwardly shape and imprint his volition and action.[19] In this fundamental principle of Thomas Aquinas is summed up the whole doctrine of prudence; in it the joint significance of all the ideas and figures of speech put forward heretofore becomes apparent, figures by which Thomas sets forth, step by step, the precedence of prudence.

The same idea is expressed in the liturgy of the Church in the following manner, in the words of prayer: *Deus, qui errantibus, ut in viam possint redire justitiae, veritatis tuae lumen ostendis*—God, Thou showest the erring the light of Thy truth, that they may return to the way of justice.[20] Truth, then, is the prerequisite of justice. Whoever rejects truth, whether natural or supernatural, is really "wicked" and beyond conversion. And from the realm of "natural" philosophizing, the realm which the supernatural "presupposes and perfects," we may call to mind Goethe's saying: "All laws and rules of conduct may ultimately be reduced to a single one: to truth." [21]

We incline all too quickly to misunderstand Thomas Aquinas's words about "reason perfected in the cognition of truth." "Reason" means to him nothing other than "regard for and openness to reality," and "acceptance of reality." And "truth" is to him nothing other than the unveiling and revelation of reality, of both natural and supernatural reality. Reason "perfected in the cognition of truth" is therefore the receptivity of the human spirit, to which the revelation of reality, both natural and supernatural reality, has given substance.

Certainly prudence is the standard of volition and action; but the standard of prudence, on the other hand, is the *ipsa res*,[22] the "thing itself," the objective reality of being. And therefore the pre-eminence of prudence signifies first of all the direction of volition and action toward truth; but finally it signifies the directing of volition and action toward objective reality. The good is prudent beforehand; but that is prudent which is in keeping with reality.

2. Knowledge of Reality and the Realization of the Good

THE PRE-EMINENCE of prudence means that realization of the good presupposes knowledge of reality. He alone can do good who knows what things are like and what their situation is. The pre-eminence of prudence means that so-called "good intention" and so-called "meaning well" by no means suffice.[1] Realization of the good presupposes that our actions are appropriate to the real situation, that is to the concrete realities which form the "environment" of a concrete human action; and that we therefore take this concrete reality seriously, with clear-eyed objectivity.

The prudent decisions, which, when realized, shape our free action, are fed from two sources: "It is necessary for the prudent man to know both the universal principles of reason and the singulars with which ethical action is concerned."[2]

The universal principles of practical intellect are given man through synderesis.* Thus these principles permeate all concrete decisions just as the highest principles of speculative reason permeate all specific judgments. In the dictates of natural conscience the most generalized cognition of the essence of the

---

* That part of conscience which concerns the most general and fundamental naturally apprehended principles of ethical conduct, and which therefore may be designated as innate conscience, or natural conscience, or primary conscience.

good becomes an imperative. "That the good must be loved and made reality"—this sentence (with what follows directly from it) is the message given us by natural conscience. It expresses the common goals of all human action.[3]—The "infused" prudence of the Christian presupposes, moreover, the three theological virtues of faith, hope, and charity.[4] In these three the Christian becomes aware that participation in the life of the Trinitarian God is the supernal goal of Christian existence.

Prudence, however, is not concerned directly with the ultimate—natural and supernatural—ends of human life, but with the means to these ends.[5] The special nature of prudence is not the presence in the mind of "universal principles" (although it is necessary for those principles to be present if one is to make prudent decisions: *synderesis movet prudentiam*;[6] and although the theological virtues are an indispensable foundation to Christian prudence). The special nature of prudence is its concern with the realm of "ways and means" and down-to-earth realities.

The living unity, incidentally, of synderesis and prudence is nothing less than the thing we commonly call "conscience."

Prudence, or rather perfected practical reason which has developed into prudence, is distinct from "synderesis" in that it applies to specific situations. We may, if we will, call it the "situation conscience." Just as the understanding of principles is necessary to specific knowledge, so natural conscience is the prerequisite and the soil for the concrete decisions of the "situation conscience,"[7] and in these decisions natural conscience first comes to a definite realization.

It is well, therefore, to remember, as we consider the foregoing and the following comments, that the word "conscience" is intimately related to and well-nigh interchangeable with the word "prudence."[8]

As the "right disposition" of practical reason, prudence looks two ways, just as does practical reason itself. It is cognitive and deciding. Perceptively it is turned toward reality, "imperatively" toward volition and action. But the cognitive aspect is prior and sets a standard; decision, which in its turn sets a standard for volition and action, receives, as something secondary and subordinate, its own standard from cognition. The decree of prudence is, as Thomas says, a "directing cognition"; [9] prudent decision rests upon the revaluation of preceding true cognitions. (This primary and fundamental cognitive aspect of prudence is, incidentally, confirmed by the direct meaning of the Latin con-scientia, which includes knowledge [scientia]; and as we have said, conscience and prudence mean, in a certain sense, the same thing.)

Prudence, however, is not only cognition, not only knowing what is what. The prime thing is that this knowledge of reality must be transformed into the prudent decision which takes effect directly in its execution. Prudence is immediately directed toward concrete realization; hence the difference between knowledge as viewed by moral science, including "casuistic" moral science, and knowledge as viewed by prudence. It is important not to mistake these two forms of ethical knowledge for one another. We shall return to this subject later.

The formal "mechanism" of that transformation of true knowledge into prudent decisions is a matter I have dealt with elsewhere. [10] The stages of the transformation are: deliberation, judgment, decision. In the receptive-perceptive attitude of deliberation and judgment is represented the cognitive character of prudence (prudentia secundum quod est cognoscitiva), while the last stage represents the imperative character (secundum quod est praeceptiva). [11]

The various modes of imperfection in that transformation of true cognitions into prudent decisions represent various types of imprudence.

For example, the person who plunges head over heels into decision and action, without proper consideration and without well-founded judgment, is being imprudent in the mode of thoughtlessness.[12] The phrase that comes to our minds in this connection is that of "energetic promptness," and we are not inclined to feel it as blameworthy. It is therefore well to remember that there are two ways of being "swift" and "slow": in deliberation and in action. Thomas says, as did the Greeks[13] before him: In deliberation we may hesitate; but a considered act must be performed swiftly.[14] Moreover, Thomas considers the capacity for instantly grasping an unexpected situation, and deciding with extreme quick-wittedness, to be one of the components of perfect prudence. *Solertia*, clear-sighted objectivity in the face of the unexpected, is expressly listed in the *Summa Theologica* as one of the prerequisites without which prudence remains imperfect.[15]

A second mode of imprudence is irresoluteness.[16] It violates and ruptures at another, at the truly decisive point, the path of transformation of true knowledge into the "imperative" of prudence. It leads to deliberation and judgment tumbling uselessly into futility instead of pouring usefully into the finality of a decision. But the true "praise" of prudence lies in decision which is directed straight toward application in action.[17]

Co-ordinate with the two aspects of prudence (the one directed toward objective reality and the other toward realization of the good) is the double set of prerequisites to which the perfection of prudence is bound. We must now speak of these prerequisites, and shall turn first to those concerning "prudence as cognition."

"Prudence as cognition," as cognition of the concrete situation of concrete action, includes above all the ability to be still in order to attain objective perception of reality. There is in addition the patient effort of experience (*experimentum*),[18] which cannot be evaded or replaced by any arbitrary, short-circuiting resort to "faith"—let alone by the "philosophical" point of view which confines itself to seeing the general rather than the particular.

It is true that every Christian receives in baptism, along with the new life of friendship with God, a supernatural "infused" prudence. But, says Thomas, this prudence granted to every Christian is limited solely to what is necessary for his eternal salvation; there is, however, a different, "fuller" prudence, not immediately granted in baptism, which enables a man "to make provision for himself and for others, not only in matters necessary for salvation, but also in all relating to human life."[19] This is that prudence in which supernatural grace has united with the "prerequisite" of a naturally perfected ability. There is, in the *Summa Theologica*, a sentence which is, incidentally, extremely comforting: "Those who need to be guided by the counsel of others, are able, if they have grace, to take counsel for themselves in this point at least, that they require the counsel of others and can distinguish good from evil counsel."[20] This is a statement which gives its due to the higher eminence of that "fuller" prudence. We must, however, guard against the misunderstanding that Thomas is speaking here of a pre-eminence of natural and "acquired" prudence over supernatural and "infused" prudence; rather, he means the pre-eminence of that "fuller" prudence in which the natural *and* the supernatural, the acquired *and* the given, are combined in a felicitous, in a literally "graced" unity.

The attitude of "silent" contemplation of reality: this is the key prerequisite for the perfection of prudence as cognition, which perfection in turn involves three elements, namely: *memoria, docilitas, solertia.*

Memoria—memory—here means more than the capacity for recollection which we have, so to speak, by nature. Nor has it anything to do with any "mnemo-technical" capacity not to

14

forget. The good memory which enters into the perfection of prudence means nothing less than "true-to-being" memory.

For the virtue of prudence resides in this: that the objective cognition of reality shall determine action; that the truth of real things shall become determinative. This truth of real things, however, is contained in the true-to-being memory. The true-to-being character of memory means simply that it "contains" in itself real things and events as they really are and were. The falsification of recollection by the assent or negation of the will is memory's worst foe; for it most directly frustrates its primary function: to be a "container" of the truth of real things. (In terms of this meaning of memory St. Augustine's often misunderstood *analogia trinitatis*[21] becomes a good deal plainer; to him memory is the spiritual proto-reality from which thought and volition take their origin; and thus it seems to him an image of God the Father, from whom the Word and the Holy Spirit proceed.)

Thomas adduces true-to-being memory as the first prerequisite for the perfection of prudence;[22] and indeed this factor is the most imperiled of all. Nowhere else is the danger so great as here, at the deepest root of the spiritual-ethical process, the danger that the truth of real things will be falsified by the assent or negation of the will. The peril is the greater for its being so imperceptible. There is no more insidious way for error to establish itself than by this falsification of the memory through slight retouches, displacements, discolorations, omissions, shifts of accent. Nor can such falsification be quickly detected by the probing conscience, even when it applies itself to this task. The honesty of the memory can be ensured only by a rectitude of the whole human being which purifies the most hidden roots of volition. Here it becomes apparent how greatly prudence, upon which all virtue depends, is in its turn dependent at its very fundaments on the totality of the other virtues, and above all on the virtue of justice. We shall return to the subject of this reciprocal dependence, for each side of the equation deserves analysis.

We see, then, that more is at stake here than "psychology"; it is, rather, the metaphysics of the ethical person that is involved.

It therefore becomes apparent that the classically Christian concept of the "virtue of prudence" is a far cry from the ordinary idea of it as knowledge of what to do in a given situation, a knowledge acquired without any great difficulty. The virtue of prudence, too, is a *bonum arduum*, a "steep good."

"No man is altogether self-sufficient in matters of prudence";[23] without *docilitas* there is no perfect prudence. *Docilitas*, however, is of course not the "docility" and the simple-minded zealousness of the "good pupil." Rather, what is meant is the kind of open-mindedness which recognizes the true variety of things and situations to be experienced and does not cage itself in any presumption of deceptive knowledge. What is meant is the ability to take advice, sprung not from any vague "modesty," but simply from the desire for real understanding (which, however, necessarily includes genuine humility). A closed mind and know-it-allness are fundamentally forms of resistance to the truth of real things; both reveal the incapacity of the subject to practice that silence which is the absolute prerequisite to all perception of reality.

Solertia is a "perfected ability," by virtue of which man, when confronted with a sudden event, does not close his eyes by reflex and then blindly, though perhaps boisterously, take random action. Rather, with the aid of *solertia* he can swiftly, but with open eyes and clear-sighted vision, decide for the good, avoiding the pitfalls of injustice, cowardice, and intemperance. Without this virtue of "objectivity in unexpected situations," perfect prudence is not possible.

In saying this, more is predicated than may be immediately apparent. Whoever has some understanding of the physico-spiritual structure of man knows to what extent physical and psychical health is necessary for the perfected ability of *solertia*, especially in that realm which is the site of neurosis, where it both originates and can be overcome. (And that realm—here we have one of the strange ambiguities of the human soul—in its depths, so removed from consciousness, is shaped and permeated by properly ethical decisions, that is, by freedom.) Here again, then, as in so many other things,'we see the high and austere demands which the classical Christian doctrine of prudence makes upon physical alertness and health, and upon "trained" physico-spiritual energies. [24]

One marginal note: The "nimbleness" in response to new situations, which is included in *solertia*, is in no way akin to fickleness; not unless we were to regard a closed mind and resistance to the truth of real things, all of which are of ever-changing form, as tokens of high-mindedness. In saying this, however, we assume that this nimbleness serves the *finis totius vitae*,[25] the genuine and immutable end of human life, and that these ever-changing forms are compatible with the truth of real things. [26]

Trueness-to-being of memory, open-mindedness, clear-sighted objectivity in unexpected circumstances: these are qualities of mind of the prudent man.

All three are focused upon what is "already" real, upon things past and present, things and situations which are "just so and no different," and which in their actuality bear the seal of a certain necessariness.

The prudent man who issues imperatives, makes resolutions and decisions, however, fixes his attention precisely upon what has "not yet" been realized, what is still to be realized. The first prerequisite for the perfection of "prudence as imperative" is, therefore, *providentia*, foresight.[27] By this is meant the capacity to estimate, with a sure instinct for the future, whether a particular action will lead to the realization of the goal.

At this point the element of uncertainty and risk in every moral decision comes to light. In the decisions of prudence, which by the very nature of prudence are concerned with things concrete, contingent, and future (*singularia, contingentia, futura*), there cannot be that certainty which is possible in a theoretical conclusion. This is what the casuists fail to understand. But since prudence is after all an "intellectual virtue," shall we not also ascribe to its decisions "the certitude of truth" (*certitudo veritatis*)? To this suggestion Thomas Aquinas responds: "*non potest certitudo prudentiae tanta esse quod omnino solicitudo tollatur*"—the certitude of prudence cannot be so great as completely to remove all anxiety.[28] A profound statement, this! Man, then, when he comes to a decision, cannot ever be sufficiently prescient nor can he wait until logic affords him absolute certainty. If he waited for that, he would never come to a decision; he would remain in a state of inconclusiveness, unless he chose to make shift with a deceptive certitude. The prudent man does not expect certainty where it cannot exist, nor on the other hand does he deceive himself by false certainties.[29]

The decisions of prudence and the "intuitions" of *providentia* (which, incidentally, Thomas considers to be the most important component of perfect prudence—he points out in fact that the name, *prudentia*, stems from *providentia*)[30] nevertheless receive "practical" assurance and reinforcement from several sources: from the experience of life as it has been lived; from the alertness and healthiness of the instinctive capacity for evaluation; from the daring and humble hope that the paths to man's genuine goals cannot be closed to him; from rectitude of volition and of ultimate "intention"; from the grace of direct and mediated divine guidance.

———

There are two manners in which man can fail to meet the demands included in the virtue of prudence.

First of all, by an actual failure and lagging behind, by the nonfulfillment of the active prerequisites of prudence. Thoughtlessness and indecisiveness, of which we have already spoken, thus come under the heading of imprudence; so also do negligence and blindness to the concrete realities which surround our actions; likewise remissness in decision. There is one thing which is common to all these forms of prudence: something is "lacking." There is a *defectus,* an *absence* of a needed quality. There is a "lack" of proper consideration, of well-founded judgment, of vigorous final decisiveness. We are astonished, and yet to some extent we understand, when Thomas Aquinas discovers that these imprudences of "omission" have their origin in unchastity,[31] in that surrender to the goods of the sensual world which splits the power of decision in two.[32]

It is, on the other hand, astonishing, surprising as a flash of lightning, but also as illuminating, to observe the manner in which Thomas traces the second group of imprudences to a common origin. But let us first discuss this other mode of imprudence. It differs from that "lack" which is the common element of thoughtlessness, indecisiveness, and negligence in the way that a dishonest affirmation differs from negation, that an apparent similarity differs from simple oppositeness. It is the difference between faulty prudence and, so to speak, "plain" imprudence. In the *quaestio* in which he treats of the false prudences[33] Thomas speaks first of the "prudence of the flesh." Instead of serving the true end of all of human life,[34] this prudence is directed solely toward the goods of the body and is, according to the Epistle to the Romans (8, 6f.), "death" and "the enemy of God." But then he devotes several articles[35] to discussing "cunning."

Cunning (*astutia*) is the most characteristic form of false prudence. What is meant by this is the insidious and unobjective temperament of the intriguer who has regard only for "tactics," who can neither face things squarely nor act straight-forwardly. In the letters of the Apostle Paul this idea of *astutia* occurs several times in a contrast which helps to clarify it, for it is opposed to "making the truth publicly known" (*manifesta-tio veritatis*, II Cor. 4, 2) and to the purity of unclouded "innocence" (*simplicitas*, II Cor. 11, 3). The same concept of *simplicitas* recurs in the legend of this book: "If thy eye is single, the whole of thy body will be lit up" (Matt. 6, 22).

There can be false and crooked ways leading even to right goals. The meaning of the virtue of prudence, however, is primarily this: that not only the end of human action but also the means for its realization shall be in keeping with the truth of real things. This in turn necessitates that the egocentric "interests" of man be silenced in order that he may perceive the truth of real things, and so that reality itself may guide him to the proper means for realizing his goal. On the other hand, the meaning, or rather the folly, of cunning consists in this: that the loquacious and therefore unhearing bias of the "tacti-cian" (only he who is silent can hear) obstructs the path of realization, blocks it off from the truth of real things. "Nor should a good end be pursued by means that are false and counterfeit but by such as are true," says Thomas.[36] Here there comes to light the affinity of prudence and of the clear-eyed virtue of magnanimity. Insidiousness, guile, craft, and concupis-cence are the refuge of small-minded and small-souled persons. Of magnanimity, however, Thomas declares in the *Summa Theologica*[37] and Aristotle in the *Nicomachean Ethics*[38] that it prefers in all things to act openly.

Astonishing, as we have said, and of a profundity scarcely to be plumbed, is the statement of Thomas Aquinas that all these false prudences and superprudences arise from covetousness and are by nature akin to it. [39]

This statement once again casts a dazzling new light upon the virtue of prudence itself and the fundamental human attitude operating within that virtue. It includes the unspoken axiom that prudence is specially opposed to covetousness. As though an explosive charge had opened a new path, there is suddenly revealed a connection between various trains of ideas which previously seemed to have no connection.

"Covetousness" here means more than the disorderly love of money and property. Covetousness here means (as Thomas says in a phrase of Gregory the Great's)[40] immoderate straining for all the possessions which man thinks are needed to assure his own importance and status (*altitudo, sublimitas*). Covetousness means an anxious senility,[41] desperate self-preservation, overriding concern for confirmation and security. Need we say how utterly contrary such an attitude is to the fundamental bent of prudence; how impossible the informed and receptive silence of the subject before the truth of real things, how impossible just estimate and decision is, without a youthful spirit of brave trust and, as it were, a reckless tossing away of anxious self-preservation, a relinquishment of all egoistic bias toward mere confirmation of the self; how utterly, therefore, the virtue of prudence is dependent upon the constant readiness to ignore the self, the limberness of real humility and objectivity?

Now at last we see how closely and directly prudence and justice are linked. "Now among all the moral virtues it is justice wherein the use of right reason"—that is, of prudence—"appears chiefly. . . . Hence the undue use of reason appears chiefly in the vices opposed to justice, the chief of which is covetousness."[42] Whoever looks only at himself and therefore does not permit the truth of real things to have its way can be neither just nor brave nor temperate—but above all he cannot be *just*. For the foremost requirement for the realization of justice is that man turn his eyes away from himself. It is not by chance that in everyday talk the ideas of partiality and injustice come to almost the same thing. [43]

Prudence, then, is the mold and mother of all virtues, the circumspect and resolute shaping power of our minds which transforms knowledge of reality into realization of the good. It holds within itself the humility of silent, that is to say, of unbiased perception; the trueness-to-being of memory; the art of receiving counsel; alert, composed readiness for the unexpected. Prudence means the studied seriousness and, as it were, the filter of deliberation, and at the same time the brave boldness to make final decisions. It means purity, straightforwardness, candor, and simplicity of character; it means standing superior to the utilitarian complexities of mere "tactics."

Prudence is, as Paul Claudel says,[44] the "intelligent prow" of our nature which steers through the multiplicity of the finite world toward perfection.

In the virtue of prudence the ring of the active life is rounded out and closed, is completed and perfected; for man, drawing on his experience of reality, acts in and upon reality, thus realizing himself in decision and in act. The profundity of this concept is expressed in the strange statement of Thomas Aquinas that in prudence, the commanding virtue of the "conduct" of life, the happiness of active life is essentially comprised. [45]

Prudence is that illumination of moral existence which, according to one of the wisest books of the East, is a thing denied to every man who "looks at himself."[46]

There is a gloomy type of resoluteness, and a bright type. Prudence is the brightness of the resoluteness of that man who "acts truth" (John 3, 21).

3. Delimitations and Contrasts

THE CLASSICAL Christian doctrine of the meaning and the rank of prudence is clearly opposed to all varieties of irrationalism and voluntarism. We need scarcely waste a word on this matter.

Man's free and responsible actions derive their form, if they are "right" and good, not from the darkness but from the light. "The first thing that is demanded of an active man is that he know."[1] But knowing implies that reality stands, bright and clear, in the human mind. "The good presupposes the true." [2] And truth is the contrary of all obscuring darkness; it means "to be manifest." [3]

On the other hand, we read elsewhere: "The first act of the will is not due to the direction of reason, but to the instigation of nature or of a higher cause."[4] The bright realm of free human action, dominated by knowledge, is bordered on all sides by darkness, by the darkness of nature's part within ourselves and by the deeper, impenetrable darkness of the immediate divine governance of our volition and our actions. These two realms are dark only to us; in reality they are irradiated by the infinite brightness of divine knowledge and providence. Of this brightness the Holy Scriptures say that it is an "unapproachable light" (I Tim. 6, 15). And Aristotle declares that our reason compares to it "as the eye of night birds to the light of the day." [5]

Moreover, the truth is the good of our knowing mind,[6] upon which the mind fixes itself by nature;[7] it is not granted to the mind to choose or not to choose that good (truth!) on the basis, again, of knowledge. The finite mind does not comprehend itself so profoundly, and does not have such power over itself, that it follows only its own light. Nor does it stand in a superior manner above real things, like a general holding inspection. Rather, it is by nature driven and compelled to know the truth of real things. This drive, which it is beyond the power of reason to oppose, proceeds along a path encompassed by that dark light which always girds and hems the bright outline of our autonomous freedom.

Nevertheless, for this area of free activity the principle remains that: *Bonum hominis est "secundum rationem esse"*— The good of man consists in being in accord with reason.[8] Once more we must add what cannot be said too often: that here the word "reason" comprises all modes of perceiving reality, and that above all the "reason" of Christians perceives also the realities of faith.

There is a type of moral preaching closely akin to voluntarism, but held by many to be particularly "Christian," which interprets man's moral activity as the sum of isolated usages, practices of virtue and omissions. This misinterpretation has as its unfortunate result the separation of moral action from its roots in the cognition of reality and from the living existences of living human beings. The preachers of such "moralism" do not know or do not want to know—but more especially they keep others from knowing—that the good, which alone is in accord with the nature of man and of reality, shines forth only in prudence. Prudence alone, that is, accords with reality. Hence, we do not achieve the good by slavishly and literally following certain prescriptions which have been blindly and arbitrarily set forth. Such moralists would be utterly baffled by the following sentence of Thomas Aquinas: "If there were temperance in the sensual appetite and there were not prudence in the reason, then the temperance would not be a virtue";[9] or the similar assertion of Gregory the Great: "If the other virtues did not accomplish their ends with prudence, they can in no wise be virtues."[10] Now prudence means, as we have already stated many times, nothing less than the directing cognition of reality. Out of this cognition good acts are "born";[11] otherwise they are not born at all. The decisions of prudence embody the duties enforced on us by things as they are; in these decisions true cognition of reality is perfected for the purpose of realizing the good.

Man's good actions take place in confrontation with reality. The goodness of concrete human action rests upon the transformation of the truth of real things; of the truth which must be won and perceived by regarding the *ipsa res*,[12] reality itself.

Now, the realities which surround man's concrete activity are of an almost infinite variety, *quasi infinitae diversitatis*.[13] And above all man himself—in this distinguishing himself from animals—is "a being of manifold and diverse activities; precisely by virtue of its rank in the order of being is the soul of man directed toward infinite variety."[14]

Since this is so, "the good of man changes in multifold fashion, according to the various conditions of men and the times and places, and similar factors."[15] However, the goals of human action do not change, nor do man's basic directions. For every "condition" of man, at all times and places, he is under obligation to be just and brave and temperate.

Yet the specific ways of accomplishing this unchanging obligation may take a thousand different forms. Of justice, of fortitude, and of temperance this is true: "Each of these is accomplished in various ways, and not in the same way for all."[16] In the *Summa Theologica* we read: "But the means to the end, in human concerns, far from being fixed, are of manifold variety according to the variety of persons and affairs."[17]

It must, however, be noted that Thomas, speaking of the performance of man's proper duties to be just (in which category falls his obedience to the laws of Church and State), remarks that these in particular are most independent of changes in situations and are therefore most likely to be fixed once and for all. [18]

Out of the very human desire to secure and comprehend, to determine, limit, and fix precisely, there arose almost of necessity man's efforts to "order" the limitless variety of modes for achieving the good, to render it surveyable by the longitudes and latitudes of abstract rational measurement. One result of this effort is casuistry, which is the branch—and often the main trunk—of ethics which has as its aim the construction, analysis, and evaluation of individual "cases."

It is all too easy to favor a certain vagueness and recklessness in concrete ethical decisions and to smile in one's sleeve at casuistry—especially if one has never been confronted with the necessity of judging the concrete ethical actions of actual human beings from a judgment seat, as it were. (It is no accident that casuistry derives from the practice of law, nor that it was originally meant as an aid for confessors.)

Nevertheless, casuistry presents its own kind of peril, owing to that persistent human desire to achieve security. The difficulty is not that no ultimate fulfillment can bless this earthly state of ours, since it is a state of being-on-the-way. It is rather that the striving for certainty and security can gravitate, by virtue of its own direction and its natural inclination, into the degenerate, anti-natural state of nonhuman rigidity. Indeed, this danger is all the greater the more powerfully the desire for certainty is concerned with the decision-making center of the spiritual person.

Casuistry falls into this trap the very moment it claims to be more than a (probably indispensable) makeshift, an aid for sharpening judgment, a technique for temporary approximation, and more than the manipulation of a lifeless model. Anyone who mistook the artificial coloring of this model for the flesh and blood of reality itself would deceive himself far more, and far more dangerously, than would a young doctor, say, who thought the models and mechanisms of his classroom represented absolute standards for the diagnosis and treatment of real diseases.

Casuistry, then, must be regarded as no more than a highly useful, and probably necessary, aid; certainly not as an absolute standard for making ethical judgments and performing concrete ethical actions. To confound model and reality, to put too great a· valuation on casuistry, is equivalent to misunderstanding the meaning and rank of the virtue of prudence. It is again no coincidence that casuistry has usurped a greater and greater place in moral theology the more that the classical Christian doctrine of prudence has been thrust into the background and has fallen into oblivion. The complexion of a number of popular textbooks on moral theology, written during the (very slowly vanishing) nineteenth century, makes the state of affairs abundantly clear: that along with the doctrine of the virtues in general, comprehension of the nature and supremacy of the first cardinal virtue had been lost. Yet this very understanding was central to the ethics of Thomas Aquinas, and kept it free of that embarrassing, excitable, omniscient, and all-intruding pedantry, that constant proliferation of warnings and interdictions. The doctrine of the pre-eminence of prudence lays the ground for the manly and noble attitude of restraint, freedom, and affirmation which marks the moral theology of the "universal teacher" of the Church.

The immediate criterion for concrete ethical action is solely the imperative of prudence in the person who has the decision to make. This standard cannot be abstractly construed or even calculated in advance; abstractly here means: outside the particular situation. The imperative of prudence is always and in essence a decision regarding an action to be performed in the "here and now." By their very nature such decisions can be made only by the person confronted with decision. No one can be deputized to make them. No one else can make them in his stead. Similarly, no one can be deputized to take the responsibility which is the inseparable companion of decision. No one else can assume this burden. The strict specificity of ethical action is perceptible only to the living experience of the person required to decide.[19] He alone has access to the totality of *singularia circa quae sunt operationes*,[20] that is to say, to the totality of concrete realities which surround the concrete action, to the "state" of the person himself and the condition of the here and the now.[21]

The statements of moral theology, including those of casuistry, necessarily remain general. They can never take hold of a real and whole "here and now" for the reason that only the person really engaged in decision experiences (or at least *can* experience) the concrete situation with its need for concrete action. He alone. This is not to deny that casuistic reasoning can more or less approach the real situation in which decision is called for. It will come all the closer, the more it deals with the attainment of *justice*. Nevertheless, real concreteness remains accessible only to immediate, the most immediate, experience. Thus all the knowledge of casuists, and the knowledge of moral theology in general, by no means suffice to guarantee the goodness of a concrete action. No matter how much moral theology "goes into details," such wisdom alone does not make a man "prudent" in the sense of the first cardinal virtue. And any moral theology becomes truer and more genuine, and above all more capable of dealing with life, the more it expressly renounces such a claim. The guarantee of the goodness of concrete human action is given solely by the virtue of prudence. It is exclusively the business of prudence "to form a right judgment concerning individual acts, exactly as they are to be done here and now."[22]

———

There is no way of grasping the concreteness of a man's ethical decisions from outside. But no, there is a certain way, a single way: that is through the love of friendship. A friend, and a *prudent* friend, can help to shape a friend's decision. He does so by virtue of that love which makes the friend's problem his own, the friend's ego his own (so that after all it is not entirely "from outside"). For by virtue of that oneness which love can establish he is able to visualize the concrete situation calling for decision, visualize it from, as it were, the actual center of responsibility. Therefore it is possible for a friend—only for a friend and only for a *prudent* friend—to help with counsel and direction to shape a friend's decision or, somewhat in the manner of a judge, help to reshape it.

Such genuine and prudent loving friendship (*amor amicitiae*)—which has nothing in common with sentimental intimacy, and indeed is rather imperiled by such intimacy—is the *sine qua non* for genuine spiritual guidance. For only this empowers another to offer the kind of direction which—almost!—conforms to the concrete situation in which the decision must be made.

Human activity has two basic forms: doing (*agere*) and making (*facere*). Artifacts, technical and artistic, are the "works" of making. We ourselves are the "works" of doing.

And prudence is the perfection of the ability to do, whereas "art" (in St. Thomas's sense)[23] is perfection of the ability to make. "Art" is the "right reason" of making (*recta ratio factibilium*); prudence is the "right reason" of doing (*recto ratio agibilium*).

The exaggerated importance given to casuistry stems in large part from disregard of this distinction between prudence and the technique of "art," the distinction between doing and making, between deeds and works.

The ethical deeds of man are not more or less fixed manual techniques, whose end is the shaping of some work, but steps toward self-realization. The human self, which grows toward perfection by accomplishing the good, is a "work" that surpasses all preconceived blueprints based upon man's own calculations. Ethical growth takes place in the course of our replies, appropriate to each given case, to the reality outside us which is not made by ourselves. The essence of that reality is the ever-changing diversity of growth and decay, not permanent being (only God is who He is). This reply appropriate to each given case can be given only by the virtue of prudence. There is no "technique" of the good, no "technique" of perfection. "Casuistry, on the contrary, carried to excess, substitutes techniques and prescriptions for the infinite suppleness which the virtue of prudence must retain in the face of the complexities of the ethical life,"[24] as we read in a French commentary to the *Summa Theologica*.

The man who does good follows the lines of an architectural plan which has not been conceived by himself and which he does not understand as a whole, nor in all of its parts. This architectural plan is revealed to man from moment to moment. In each case he sees only a tiny segment of it, as through a narrow crack. Never, so long as he is in the state of "being-on-the-way," will the concrete architectural plan of his own self become visible to him in its rounded and final shape.

Paul Claudel defines conscience—which, as we have said, is in a certain sense equivalent to prudence itself—as "the patient beacon which does not delineate the future, but only the immediate."[25]

A moral theology which relies too much upon casuistry necessarily becomes a "science of sins" instead of a doctrine of virtues, or a theory of the Christian idea of man.[26] It soon becomes reduced to an endless determining of the boundary beyond which sins are "mortal" and this side of which sins are "venial." If such a casuistic doctrine of sin is combined with the moralism of isolated "observances" and "abstentions"—and it is indeed akin to this moralism—there arises that phenomenon (which was, after all, not completely invented by Nietzsche) of a rather vindictive and insubstantial nay-saying which serves at best to prey upon the consciences of the immature, but is of no use as a standard for real life.

A merely casuistic moral theology assumes the immaturity of human beings. Moreover, it intensifies and perpetuates this immaturity. "Once we have arrived at casuistry, the next consequence is that decisions in questions of conscience are lifted from the conscience of the individual and transferred to the authority of the experts" (Linsenmann).[27]

The virtue of prudence, on the contrary—being the perfected ability to make decisions in accordance with reality—is the quintessence of ethical maturity (of which, of course, teachability is a great component). And the pre-eminence of prudence over justice, fortitude, and temperance means simply that without maturity truly moral life and action is not possible.

If, then, prudence is truly the mold and mother of all moral virtue, then it is likewise true that it is impossible to educate a person to justice, fortitude, and temperance without first and simultaneously educating him to prudence. And education to prudence means: to objective estimation of the concrete situation of concrete activity, and to the ability to transform this cognition of reality into concrete decision.

The classical Christian doctrine of the pre-eminence of the virtue of prudence is essentially opposed to all falsifying, moralistic, or casuistic regimentation of the person who is called upon to make decisions.

The first of the cardinal virtues is not only the quintessence of ethical maturity, but in so being is also the quintessence of moral freedom.

4. Prudence and Charity

"NO MORAL VIRTUE is possible without prudence."[1]But in contrast to this we read: "Without the moral virtues there is no prudence."[2]Both these sentences are to be found in Thomas Aquinas's treatises on prudence. Only the prudent man, then, can be just, brave, and temperate; yet he who is not already just, brave, and temperate cannot be prudent.

How can the first sentence be compatible with the second, which seems to run counter to it?

A vague reply that both are simultaneously possible is not uncommon, but is no more satisfactory than the other explication we hear frequently: that these sentences are meant to convey the idea that the ethical life is "organic" and constitutes a closed circulatory system. Such exegesis wrongs the clarity of outline and the precision which is peculiar to the thinking of the "universal teacher." Either prudence gives rise to the moral virtues, or these virtues engender prudence; both statements cannot be true and real in one and the same sense. When the snake curls itself into a ring, it is always the head that bites the tail, not vice versa. Thus the "both are simultaneously possible" and the "closed circulatory system" are fundamentally non-sense, mere subterfuges for thinking that lacks decisiveness and exactitude.

It is not the purpose or the business of the virtue of prudence to discover the goals, or rather the goal, of life, and to determine the fundamental inclinations of the human being. Rather, the purpose of prudence is to determine the proper roads to that goal and the suitable outlet in the here and now for those fundamental inclinations.

To know the ultimate goals of one's own life is not and cannot be the fruit of an ability still to be acquired and perfected in this very "life." The goals are present. No one is ignorant of the fact that he must love the good and accomplish it. Everyone knows—expressly or not—that the good most characteristic of the nature of man is "to be according to reason"³—that is, to be according to the reality which man himself is and which surrounds him. And there is no one who needs to be told that he ought to be just and brave and temperate. This is self-evident, and calls for no deliberation. The reflections and the conclusions of prudence are directed solely toward the actual realization of justice, fortitude, and temperance.

This concrete realization, however, could not do justice to reality, and above all could not be satisfactorily consummated, if conscious affirmation of the goal of man did not precede the efforts of prudence. That is to say, there must precede the affirmation of justice, fortitude, and temperance as the fundamental inclinations of man toward the accomplishment of the "good characteristic of his nature," of "being according to reason." Without desire for the good in general, all efforts to discover what is prudent and good here and now remain empty bustle and self-deception. The virtue of prudence presumes real seeking of the goal of man, the *intentio finis*.⁴ It therefore not only presupposes the voice of the natural conscience ("synderesis"), as we have said several times, but also the response of the will to this imperative pronouncement: primal affirmation of the good as the aim of all of one's actions. This primal affirmation, however, is nothing less than the fundamental attitude of the just, brave, and temperate man —that is to say, of the good man.⁵

Moral virtue, in so far as it signifies that basic attitude of voluntary affirmation of the good, is the fundament and precondition of prudence. But prudence in turn is the prerequisite for the appropriate realization in the here and now of that same basic attitude; the prerequisite for its effectuality. Only one who previously and simultaneously *loves* and *wants* the good can be prudent; but only one who is previously prudent can *do* good. Since, however, love of the good in its turn grows by doing good, the foundations of prudence are sunk deeper and firmer to the extent that prudence bears fruit in action.

(The original desire for the good takes its energy from the ever-pulsating momentum of that Origin in which man, answering the creative call of God, flew across the abyss which parts nothingness from existence. It is the moment with which the possible bursts with a roar into the radiant dawn of its first realization: the swift current of a stream that originating in the bright darkness of mere Nature and steadily fed by its source, crosses by the dictates of innate conscience into the realm of freedom.)

In concrete moral action cognition and will are interwoven into oneness. Both strands have their beginnings far beyond the narrow realm of self-understanding. And the "pattern" as well as the rule which governs their weaving into a fabric very soon passes beyond the range of man's vision.[6] Yet this may be said: that the contribution which cognition and decision bring to the concrete moral act is quite different in nature from the contribution of the will. The realization of the good presumes both voluntary affirmation of the good and the decisions of prudence; but both have an entirely different relationship to the concrete good activity of man. Prudent decision is the "measure" of a concrete moral act. That is to say, the act receives from prudent decision its content, its nature, its essence, its inner truth and rightness. On the other hand, man's concrete moral actions receive their existence, their being, their real goodness, from the will's power of realization. "Making existent" is the special and the only function of volition.

This again casts light on the statement that prudence is dependent upon volitional affirmation of the good as man's goal. This is not to say that the *content* of a prudent decision is directly determined or determinable by volition and derives its substance from the will. The content of prudent decision is, rather, determined by the *ipsa res*, by reality, which is the "measure" of all cognition and decision. Desiring the good does not make a decision prudent; but real understanding and proper evaluation of the concrete situation of the concrete act does. Not voluntary affirmation of the goal, not the *intentio finis*, is the "measure" of a prudent decision. But, on the other hand, the volitional affirmation of the good "makes existent" the prudent decision, so that this decision, effectively, may obtain its contentual rightness from true cognition of reality. The will can never determine, never produce, the contentual truth of cognition and decision, and therefore can never determine or produce the quality of good action. (And on the other hand, no cognition, no matter how true, and no decision, no matter how prudent, will by itself suffice for the actual achievement of the good.)[7] But the authenticity of the desire for the goal clears the way for truth, so that truth can imprint upon will and action the seal of justness to the nature of things. An unjust will, on the other hand, prevents the truth of real things from determining the actions of man. There are depths of meaning not easily grasped in the sentence in the Epistle to the Romans that truth is held captive in the fetters of injustice (Rom. 1, 18).[8]

"Human acts are good in that they correspond to the right standard of human action. Now there is a right standard proper to the human species and peculiar to man's nature, namely right reason; and there is another, supreme and surpassing standard, which is God. Man attains right reason in prudence, which is right reason in the realm of action. But man attains God in charity." [9]

"Prudence is called the form of all the moral virtues. But the act of virtue thus established in the mean is, as it were, material in regard to the ordination to the last end. This order is conferred upon the act of virtue by the command of charity. In this sense charity is said to be the form of all the other virtues." [10]

It is, alas, only too easy for the superficial reader to float along on the unruffled surface of these statements of Thomas Aquinas, which seem transparent to the very bottom, and take no account of the depths over which their serene clarity lies.

Very often the proposition about nature presupposed and perfected by grace is cited as a self-evident "explanation." But the fact is that this expresses an almost impenetrable mystery. Moreover, the dictum primarily concerns the domain of generalities and essences, not that of immediate and concrete existence. More exactly, the accord of the natural order with the new life of friendship with God must not be construed in the sense that it is immediately "given" or realizable in smooth and "harmonious" development. We do, to be sure, incline to think in terms of such harmonies from long habit. But the writings of the great friends of God make plain, on almost every page, that the actual life of the Christian is ruled by a different kind of structural law; that life on earth, which has "not yet" attained the peace of concord, the concrete combination of the natural and the supernatural, is subjected to all sorts of liabilities to contradiction and disharmony.

Yet it is not true that the greatest liabilities of such a discord lie in the *lowest* realm of the natural life—in, say, the resistance of the sensual natural will to supernatural duty. Rather, the peril is most present in the confrontation of the *highest* natural virtue and the highest theological virtue, that is to say, in the connection of natural prudence and supernatural charity. It is not the "sinners" but the "prudent ones" who are most liable to close themselves off from the new life which has been given by grace, and to oppose it. Typically, natural prudence courts this danger by tending to restrict the realm of determinative factors of our actions to naturally experienceable realities. Christian prudence, however, means precisely the throwing open of this realm and (in faith informed by love) the inclusion of new and invisible realities within the determinants of our decisions.

It need scarcely be said that, on the other hand, the highest and most fruitful achievements of Christian life depend upon the felicitous collaboration of prudence and charity.

This collaboration is linked to the pre-eminence of charity over prudence. Prudence is the mold of the moral virtues; but charity molds even prudence itself.[11] How this molding of prudence by charity takes place in practice can scarcely be stated, for charity, being participation by grace in the life of the Trinitarian God, is in essence a gift ultimately beyond the power of man's will or reason to bestow. It is an event unfathomable in any natural way, which takes place when the three theological virtues are "infused" into our being. This, however, is certain: that all our works and being are elevated by charity to a plane which is otherwise unattainable and utterly inaccessible. For that reason, too, supernatural divine love which molds the decisions of the Christian indubitably means something far more than and far different from a mere additional "higher motivation" in the psychological sense. The divine love conferred by grace shapes from the ground up and throughout the innermost core of the most commonplace moral action of a Christian, even though that action may be "outwardly" without special distinguishing characteristics. It does so, however, in a manner that lies outside the range of ordinary psychological experience-possibilities.

In proportion to the growth of the theological virtue of love there unfolds in the man who has received grace the sevenfold gift of the Holy Spirit; in the same proportion human prudence receives, more tangibly and more audibly, the aid of the "gift of counsel," *donum consilii.* "The gift of counsel corresponds to prudence, helping and perfecting it."[12] "The human mind, from the very fact that it is directed by the Holy Spirit, is enabled to direct itself and others."[13]

But: "In the gift of the Holy Spirit, the position of the human mind is of one moved rather than of a mover."[14] And therefore here, too, there can be no question of how and how much. It would, after all, be absurd arrogance to attempt to discover the "rules" by which the Holy Spirit of God permeates man's reflections and decisions. We can at most say that the quasi-infinite variety of choices which operate in the realm of natural prudence and make any general and abstract predetermination possible, must be multiplied by an utterly new infinity in the supernatural order. This emerges clearly when we recall how incomparable and unique the life of every single saint is. Here, then, is the truest applicability of the dictum of Augustine: "Have love, and do what you will."

In the *Summa Theologica* we learn that upon a higher plane of perfection, that is the plane of charity, there is also a higher and extraordinary prudence which holds as nought all the things of this world.[15]

Does this not run completely counter to all that the "universal teacher" has said elsewhere about the nature of the first cardinal virtue? Is holding created things as nought not the exact opposite of that reverent objectivity which in the concrete situation of concrete action must attempt to recognize the "measure" of that action?

Things are nought only before God, who created them and in whose hand they are as clay in the hand of the potter. By the superhuman force of grace-given love, however, man may become one with God to such an extent that he receives, so to speak, the capacity and the right to see created things from God's point of view and to "relativize" them and see them as nought from God's point of view, *without* at the same time repudiating them or doing injustice to their nature. Growth in love is the legitimate avenue and the one and only justification for "contempt for the world."

Unlike this contempt which arises out of growth in love, all contempt for the world which springs from man's own judgment and opinions, not from the supernatural love of God, is simple arrogance, hostile to the nature of being; it is a form of pride in that it refuses to recognize the ordinary obligations which are made visible to man in created things. Only that closer union with the being of God which is nourished by love raises the blessed man beyond immediate involvement in created things.

At this point in our argument we approach a limit. Beyond that limit only the experience of the saints can offer any valid knowledge, any valid comment. We would only remind our readers how intensely the great saints loved the ordinary and commonplace, and how anxious they were lest they might have been deceived into regarding their own hidden craving for the "extraordinary" as a "counsel" of the Holy Spirit of God.

But even in that higher and extraordinary form of prudence which holds the world in contempt, there reigns unrestrictedly the same fundamental attitude upon which ordinary prudence entirely depends: the fundamental attitude of justice toward the being of things and correspondence to reality.

The eye of perfected friendship with God is aware of deeper dimensions of reality, to which the eyes of the average man and the average Christian are not yet opened. To those who have this greater love of God the truth of real things is revealed more plainly and more brilliantly; above all the super-natural reality of the Trinitarian God is made known to them more movingly and overwhelmingly.

Even supreme supernatural prudence, however, can have only the following aim: to make the more deeply felt truth of the reality of God and world the measure for will and action. Man can have no other standard and signpost than things as they are and the truth which makes manifest things as they are; and there can be no higher standard than the God who is and His truth.

And of the man who "acts truth" the Holy Scriptures (John 3, 21) tell us that he "comes to the light."

JUSTICE

"*Justice is destroyed in twofold fashion: by the false prudence of the sage and by the violent act of the man who possesses power.*"
ST. THOMAS, *On the Book of Job* [8, 1].

1. On Rights

AMONG ALL the things that preoccupy us today, there seem to be few that are not connected with justice in a very intimate fashion. A survey of current problems reveals this clearly. There is, first and foremost, one of the most urgent concerns of our times: How can genuine authority be once more established in the world? There are the problems of "human rights," of a "just war" and war crimes, of responsibility in the face of unjust commands; the right of opposition against unlawful authority; capital punishment, dueling, political strikes, equality of rights for women. Every one of these issues is, as we all know, controversial. And each one has an immediate connection with the notion of justice.

Over and above that, however, anyone who judges the realities encountered in everyday life by the standard of "justice" will clearly see that evil and suffering in our world have many names, but primarily that of "injustice." "Man's greatest and most frequent troubles depend on man's injustice more than on adversity" (Kant).[1] Consequently, when Aristotle undertakes to explain the distinctive and fundamental forms of justice, he expressly starts from what is our most familiar experience, and that is injustice. "The many forms of injustice make the many forms of justice quite clear,"[2] he says.

All that is true, yet whenever "justice" is analyzed, so vast a multitude of meanings come to mind that it is quite impossible to master them. Nevertheless there is a notion of the utmost simplicity to which that bewildering variety can be reduced.

43

Indeed, Plato already mentions it as if it were handed down by long tradition.[3] It is the notion that each man is to be given what is his due.

All just order in the world is based on this: that man give man what is his due. On the other hand, everything unjust implies that what belongs to a man is withheld or taken away from him—and, once more, not by misfortune, failure of crops, fire or earthquake, but by man.

This notion, then, the notion of the "*suum cuique*," which ever since the very earliest times became the common possession of the Western tradition through Plato, Aristotle,[4] Cicero,[5] Ambrose,[6] Augustine,[7] and, above all, Roman law,[8] will have to be discussed in what follows. More precisely, the discussion will have to be about the intentional habit that enables man to give to each one what is his. In a word, the *virtue* of justice must be investigated.

"Justice is a habit (*habitus*), whereby a man renders to each one his due with constant and perpetual will." [9]

There are, of course, other definitions of justice in the Western tradition, too. In Thomas himself there are several kinds of definition each with a different ring to it. Thus, in one place he says that justice is that whereby what is one's own is distinct from what belongs to a stranger;[10] or again: it is properly the mark of justice to establish order among things.[11] Augustine has likewise spoken of the virtue of justice in many different ways. A particular luster attaches to the following formulation: "Justice is that ordering of the soul by virtue of which it comes to pass that we are no man's servant, but servants of God alone."[12] Yet such statements are hardly intended to be proper definitions of the term. That is true only of the statement already quoted—the most sober and factual of all—which says: Justice is the virtue which enables man to give to each one what is his due.

I have just said that this idea is an extremely simple one. But that does not imply that its meaning is easily grasped and, as it were, without paying any price. For what, in fact, is each man's due? And above all, what is, generally speaking, the basis for a "*suum*"? How does anything come to belong to a person, anyway? And how does it so truly belong to him that every man and every human authority has to grant it to him and allow him to keep it?

Perhaps as a consequence of what has happened throughout the world during the past decades—and is still happening—we are now newly gifted to see what is properly involved in such a fundamental consideration. The answer is no longer self-evident; the most extreme formulations—and realizations, too—of absolute untruth have come to the fore; and thus the deepest foundations of truth are once more called in question because they are expressly attacked. It is therefore opportune and, indeed, necessary to think these matters through in a new and more radical fashion.

"If the act of justice is to give to each man his due, then the act of justice is preceded by the act whereby something becomes his due."[13] This text expresses with supreme simplicity a circumstance that is utterly fundamental. Justice is something that comes second: right comes before justice. If something is due to a man as his own, the fact of its being due to him has not come into existence through justice. "That act, by virtue of which something comes for the first time to be due to a man as *his*, cannot be an act of justice."[14]

Let us take an example. One man does a job for another; let us say he digs his garden for him. (For the purpose of our example, we assume that in performing this task he is not fulfilling a previous obligation.) By his digging, something due to him has come into being. By reason of something that he has done, something is now due to him. And that other man must give him his due. Now this act of giving is an act of justice, and it has as its condition, then, the fact that something is due to his neighbor.

Everyone is aware, however, that there are rights which do

not arise out of one's work; in other words, that man has a right to some things as his due, which has no basis in any action of his. No one, for example, doubts that a man has a right to his own life.

Now the question that arises in this connection goes deeper. It also embraces the claim based on the performance of a task: for what reason is "recompense" due a man for work done? What is the basis of this obligation? What, in the final analysis, is "the act whereby for each man something becomes his due"?

"It is through creation that the created being first comes to have his rights."[15] By virtue of creation first arises the possibility of saying: "Something is my due." This may sound rather obvious. But on the basis of it Thomas draws this surprising but compelling conclusion: "Therefore, creation itself is not an act of justice; creation is not anyone's due."[16] This means that in the relationship of God to man, there cannot be justice in the strict sense of *reddere suum cuique*: God owes man nothing. "And although God in this way pays each thing its due, yet He Himself is not the debtor."[17] This is surely a new theme. And it is something we shall have to discuss.

At this juncture it must be made clear that no obligation to do justice exists unless it has as its presupposition this idea of the due, the right, the *suum*. That is the meaning of the proposition: "Now the Just is the object of justice."[18] I must confess that it took me a number of years to grasp this point and realize it fully. Only then did I understand, and for the first time, why in the *Summa Theologica* a question, "On Right," issuing from the systematic order that preceded it, came before the treatise on justice.

So if, to the question: "How does man come to have his due," we give the answer: "By reason of creation," we have already said a good deal. Yet we have still not said the last word. The question has still not been given an answer in formal terms.

For stones, plants, and animals have also been created, yet we cannot say that they have their due in the strict sense of the word. For "being due" means something like belonging to or being the property of someone.[19] A nonspiritual being, however, cannot properly have anything belonging to it; on the contrary it, itself, belongs to someone else, for instance, to man.

The concept of "being due to," of "right," is such a primordial idea that it cannot be traced back to a prior, subordinating concept. That is to say, it can at best be described, but not defined. We can perhaps say this: Whatever is due to a person, the *suum*, is something that one man may demand of another as owing to him, and him only. And what *is* thus owing can just as well be a thing, perhaps a possession, as an action—and, indeed, not only a private action, such as not being hindered in one's private actions (be it speaking, writing, marrying, or going to church), but it can also be an act performed by another, or even the cessation of such an act—anything, for instance, that might be annoying, embarrassing, or compromising to a person's good name.

Yet the question persists: On what basis does a man have his due in such a way that it is his inalienable possession? We have nowadays become so accustomed to thinking in the categories of despotism that the great word "inalienable" almost makes us smile. This or that "inalienably" belongs to me! What can such a claim really mean? There is another, more forceful, way of stating the case. That something belongs to a man inalienably means this: the man who does not give a person what belongs to him, withholds it or deprives him of it, is really doing harm to himself; *he* is the one who actually loses something—indeed, in the most extreme case, he even destroys himself. At all events, something incomparably worse befalls him than hap-

47

pens to the one who suffers an injustice: that is how inviolable
the right is! That is how strongly the inalienability of the right
asserts itself! Socrates has formulated this point over and over
again—the person who does an injustice is "to be pitied":[20]"But
as to my own view, though it has often been expressed
already, there is no harm in my expressing it once more. I
maintain, Callicles, that it is not the most shameful of things to
be wrongfully boxed on the ears, nor again to have either my
purse or my person cut . . . any wrong done to me and mine
is at once more shameful and worse for the wrongdoer than
for me the sufferer."[21] Expressions such as this should not be
construed as simply heroic hyperbole; they are meant as a
very precise description of the condition that justice belongs
to man's true *being*. All these statements are sober characterizations of a real state of affairs: "the inalienability of right."

What is the basis, then, upon which something comes to be
the inalienable due of a person—the presupposition of justice?
First of all, the issue might be skirted by giving a less radical
answer and saying that a due can arise in many different ways;
even Thomas has given such an answer. He says:[22]"On the one
hand a thing might be due to a man on the basis of agreements,
treaties, promises, legal decisions, and so on; on the other hand,
it might be due to him on the basis of the nature of the thing,
ex ipsa natura rei ("and this is called natural right, *ius naturale*";
this is the point where the extremely complicated concept of
"natural law" is anticipated). It is true, Thomas adds a remark
of the utmost importance to this distinction: it is not exclusive;
only on the assumption that the agreement between men, private or public, does not run counter to "the nature of things"
may a settlement be the basis for an obligation to a person, that
is, of a right. "If, however, a thing of itself is contrary to
natural right, the human will cannot make it just." [23]

This is a further help in formulating our question—still the
same one—more precisely: something can truly come to be

due to me by mere agreement, for instance through a promise; so much so that a person acts against justice and is therefore to be pitied and injures himself, if he withholds it from me. On what, then, does the inalienability, even of this obligation, rest?

It is based, we must reply, on the nature of him to whom the obligation is due. There can be an obligation, in the fullest sense of the term, invulnerable and inalienable, only if the bearer of this *suum* is of such a kind that he can claim what is due to him as his right. At this point language seems only to complicate the matter and to have reached the limits of its power to express meaning clearly. This is perfectly natural and we cannot expect anything else. That is what happens when we try to make a primordial and therefore self-evident concept more intelligible.

Let us take a fictitious example: Suppose I promise my dog something. Let us assume that a sort of customary "right" had been established, that for a certain act the dog should get a reward, with the result that the dog "rightfully" considers it to be something due to him; on my part, let us suppose that I have expressly decided to reward the animal regularly in some definite way. If I were to omit doing so just once, I would, of course, be inattentive, inconstant, forgetful. But in no way would I be unjust in the proper sense. Why not? Because nothing can be inalienably due to a brute; because the presupposition of justice, as well as of injustice—namely, that a "right" in the full sense exists on the side of the other party—does not obtain. [24]

This implies, on the other hand, that we cannot state the basis of a right and, hence, of a judicial obligation, unless we have a concept of man, of human nature.[25] But what if it is claimed that there is, absolutely speaking, no human nature—"*Il n'y a pas de nature humaine*"?[26] This is, in truth, the formal justification for every exercise of totalitarian power—even though such a connection may not have entered the head of

Jean Paul Sartre, who originated this existentialist thesis. If, then, there is no human nature on the basis of which alone there is an inalienable obligation to man, how can we escape the consequence: Do whatever you think fit with man?

Man, however, is a *person*—a spiritual being, a whole unto himself, a being that exists for itself and of itself, that wills its own proper perfection. Therefore, and for *that very reason*, something *is* due to man in the fullest sense, *for that reason* he does inalienably have a *suum*, a "right" which he can plead against everyone else, a right which imposes upon every one of his partners the obligation at least not to violate it. Indeed, man's personality, "the constitution of his spiritual being by virtue of which he is master of his own actions," even requires (*requirit*), says Thomas,[27] that Divine Providence guide the personality "for his own sake." Moreover, he takes literally that marvelous expression from the Book of Wisdom: Even God Himself disposes of us "with great reverence" (*cum magna reverentia*).[28] In the same chapter of the *Summa contra Gentiles* in which this statement occurs the concept of the personality is set forth in all its elements: its freedom, imperishability, and responsibility for the whole of the world. If, on the contrary, man's personality is not acknowledged to be something wholly and entirely real, then right and justice cannot possibly be established.

Nevertheless, even establishing them in this way still does not get at their deepest roots. For how can human nature be the *ultimate* basis when it is not founded upon itself! At this point we could certainly break off any further boring into the depth. In "moderate" periods, in fact, there would be nothing against it. When the most far-reaching denials of justice take the stage, however, it is no longer enough to go back only to penultimate roots. If man is treated as though simply nothing were due to him as his right, as a *suum*—not merely because the wielding of power has become brutalized, but rather on the basis of a fully articulated theory—at such a time mere reference to the person's freedom and to human rights will obviously not carry us very far. This is simply part of the experiences of our age. Something must be said of the deepest roots of such rights. But more than words are needed. We must learn to experience as reality the knowledge that the establishment of right and justice has not received its fullest and most valid legitimation until we have gone back to the absolute foundation; and that there is no other way to make the demands of justice effective as absolute bounds set the will to power.

This means in concrete terms: Man has inalienable rights because he is created a person by the act of God, that is, an act beyond all human discussion. In the ultimate analysis, then, something is inalienably due to man because he is *creatura*. Moreover, as *creatura*, man has the absolute duty to give another his due. Kant has expressed this in the following manner: "We have a divine Sovereign, and his divine gift to man is man's right." [29]

Now a person may very well consider this to be true and may even give it his unqualified consent, but he may nevertheless discover that he himself finds it difficult to draw the conclusion that man's right is unimpeachable because he is created by God. Pious declamation on solemn occasions is not enough. Fundamental truths must constantly be pondered anew lest they lose their fruitfulness. In this lies the significance of meditation: that truth may not cease to be present and effective in the active life. Perhaps when all the consequences of a false presupposition suddenly become a direct threat men in their great terror will become aware that it is no longer possible to call back to true and effective life a truth they have allowed to become remote—just for the sake of their bare survival.

Finally, it is no longer completely fantastic to think that a day may come when not the executioners alone will deny the existence of inalienable rights of men, but when even the victims will not be able to say why it is that they are suffering injustice.

It has, I hope, become clear by now that we are not concerned with some vague need for theological trimmings, or with mere edification, but rather with the sober reflective will not to shirk "embarrassing" conclusions and to carry the question through to its ultimate meaning, the question, namely: On what basis is something inalienably due to man, and for what reason does justice first become thinkable and demonstrable as a duty, the violation of which destroys man himself?

But this is not to say that man himself is not possessor and bearer of his right, the *suum*. However true it is that the Creator in His Absoluteness is the *ultimate* foundation for the inalienability of man's rights, still man himself has dues rendered him by all others (indeed he renders dues to all others in turn). "A thing is just not only because it is willed by God, but because it is a debt due to a created being by virtue of the relationship between creature and creature." [30]

This would seem to be the place to speak briefly about one other presupposition of justice. A person may make no formal denial that another should have his due. But he may say that this is no concern of his; that as a man of action it is all the same to him whether in the realm of objective truth one thing goes or another. In other words, as Thomas says, the act of justice not only presupposes that act through which a man comes to have his due; it also presupposes the act of *prudence*, which means that the truth of real things is transposed into a decision.

It is only in terms of such a situation that it first becomes possible to conceive of one form of injustice that is extremely real, the kind of injustice that rests on man's having lost his contact with truth. To him the question as to whether a man has his due or not is absolutely and utterly irrelevant. As a result, something far more radically inhuman than formal injustice comes to the fore; for human actions are properly human because they have taken reality as their measure.[31]

We have made clear that justice can be discussed meaningfully and fruitfully only if it is regarded in the context of a complete moral doctrine. It is *one* feature in the sevenfold image of man; the part becomes fully intelligible only within the whole.

2. Duty in Relation to "The Other"

"IT IS PROPER to justice, as compared with the other virtues, to direct man in his relations with others; . . . on the other hand the other virtues perfect man only in those matters which befit him in relation to himself."[1] This text from the *Summa Theologica* has the very same meaning as the textbook adage: *"Iustitia est ad alterum"*—Justice is directed toward the other man. The difference, the separateness of the other party is intended more precisely and literally than may appear at first glance.[2]

What distinguishes justice from love[3] is just this: in the relationship of justice, men confront each other as separate "others," almost as strangers. "Justice properly speaking demands a distinction of parties."[4] Because father and child are not entirely separate individuals, because the child, instead, belongs to the father, and the father feels toward the child almost as he feels toward himself, "so between them there is not a *simpliciter iustum*, the just, simply,"[5] not justice in the strict sense. Because the loved one is not properly "someone else," there is no formal justice between those who love each other. To be just means to recognize the other *as other*; it means to give acknowledgment even where one cannot love. Justice says: That is another person, who is other than I, and who nevertheless has his own peculiar due. A just man is just,

54

therefore, because he sanctions another person in his very separateness and helps him to receive his due.

It is not superfluous, I think, to spell out every obvious stage of the argument as we have done. For nowadays "liquidation" is both concept and reality. Liquidation does not mean punishment, subjugation, conquest, or even execution. Liquidation means extermination merely on the basis of otherness. It would be unrealistic not to see that this ferment: "Whoever is different will be liquidated," works on like a poison, a constant temptation to human thought, destroying or at least menacing it.

That is why it is important to call even the elements of the concept of justice by the right name. Only when we realize what a challenge this concept presents to ordinary current thinking, is it worth while to ponder it step by step.

Once we consider the theory of justice as a development of the possibilities of human partnership, of men's relations to "the other," one sign of the erosion and growing aridity of this field in the contemporary human consciousness is the inability of our living tongue to give names to all the various possible violations of partnership enumerated and described in classical Western moral doctrine. We may venture to assert that expressions like "calumny," "malign aspersion," "backbiting," "slander," "talebearing"[6] are now in their proper meanings scarcely intelligible to most people—to say nothing of their essential flavor and expressiveness having long since grown stale and flat. What is "talebearing"? Our forebears understood by it: privately spreading evil reports about another, and to that other's friend, no less. And they maintained this was an especially grievous violation of justice, since no man can live without friends.[7] But it is obvious that today we can no longer (rather, never again) describe such an act as "talebearing." The fact that current adult speech has not maintained such a usage, that we actually do not have words for such things and many others like them, seems to me most disturbing, and thought-provoking. What term shall we use properly to render *derisio*, the act that violates justice by bringing shame to another through mockery? How designate the special form of justice that goes with it and consists in sparing another man shame?

What I have just said must appear trivial, mere "uplift," utterly unreal, to anyone coming from a world where the concept of "liquidation" is valid. And yet, does it not correspond to the reality of the give-and-take of human life that, varying with the concrete demands of constantly changing situations, one either acknowledges and grants the other his due or else curtails it, deprives him of it, withholds it? The significance of a theory of justice as a virtue lies precisely in considering these manifold ways, giving them names, ordering them, formulating them as ideal images, and making these images familiar to man's consciousness.

Justice, therefore, "consists in living one with another";[8] the just man has to deal with the other.

In this present inquiry, however, we are concerned only with the man who wants to be and should be just. Therefore, we are not concerned with "the other," but rather with "the one"; not with the one entitled to something, to whom something is due, but with the one bound by duty, the man who has to give another his due. This is the man who is brought to task by the demands of justice. The one called to justice finds himself by this very fact in the position of a debtor.

Now there are many different degrees and grades of obligation. A person owes the agreed price of an article in a different, stricter way than he is obliged to return thanks for a favor. I am more rigidly bound not to deceive my neighbor than I am obliged to greet him on the street. Thomas has noted very clearly this distinction between a demand of justice that is legally binding and a demand of justice that is (only) morally binding. I can be compelled to fulfill the first obligation;[9] carrying out the second depends only on my own sense of decency.[10] Moreover, there is a further distinction to be made between demands of justice that are only morally binding: a violation can mean that the person who commits it has done something dishonorable (if he lies, for example); but it may also mean that without being strictly dishonorable, an action has still been "unseemly" (in that it is unkind or unfriendly, for example).

What is common, however, to all these obligations proper to justice is that in every case there is a *debitum*, something owing, a debt. To be just means, then, to owe something and to pay the debt.

One remark: If justice is understood in this way, then, as we have already said, God cannot properly be called "just"—even though, on the other hand, none of the moral virtues, neither fortitude nor temperance, can be ascribed to God with greater justification than justice.[11] God is indebted to no one. "Nothing is owed to the thing created unless it be on the basis of something that pre-existed in it . . . and again if this is owing to the thing created, it will again be because of something prior to it. And since we cannot go on to infinity, we must come to something that depends only on the goodness of the divine will" (thus the *Summa Theologica*).[12] At most, God's debt is to Himself. "He renders to Himself what is due to Himself."[13] That, however, is not properly a debt and not properly justice. On this point Thomas cites the *Proslogion* of Anselm of Canterbury,[14] in which he expresses the inscrutability of the justice of God thus: "When thou dost punish the wicked, it is just; since it agrees with their deserts; and when thou dost spare the wicked, it is also just; since it befits thy Goodness."[15]

Once again: The distinguishing mark of justice is that some debt is to be paid. But am I not doing my duty whenever, in general terms, I fulfill a moral obligation?

It now comes to light that in ethics the fundamental principle of duty, of what one ought to do, of the *debitum*, has its origin in the field of justice. In the Germanic languages, as well as in Latin and Greek, there are words indicating moral obligation that do not at the same time pertain to the realm of justice. "Debt," "debit," and "to be indebted" are obviously related words. And so are "owe" and "ought." The same thing is true of the Latin words "*debere, obligatum esse.*"[16] And the Greek word ὀφειλόμενον (which means the same thing as "due, debt, duty") has been related by Plato himself to the meaning: "what has to be paid as a debt to another." [17]

This indicates that the total structure of ethics is revealed, as in a concave mirror, with clearer, sharper outline, in the structure of the act of justice. Something is here revealed that at first glance might otherwise remain hidden. "At first glance (*primo aspectui*)," says Thomas,[18] "it might seem that, as long as a partner does not come forth with a concrete claim, a person may do whatever he thinks fit." But if we consider more deeply, we will find that not only justice but every moral obligation has a personal character, the character of the commitment to the person to whom I am under an obligation. "The notion of duty which is essential to a precept appears in justice." [19]

To do the good, therefore, does not mean that a person obeys some abstract norm, an imperative without imperator. On the contrary, even though it has to do with the most private realm of one's thoughts or the disciplining of appetite, which would seem "at first glance" to belong exclusively to the individual, to do good or evil always means to give or withhold from a person I have to deal with, what is "his." "We are directed to another by all the precepts of the Decalogue" [20] —the Decalogue, which forms a comprehensive *Summa* of the whole field of moral thought.

But who is that "other one" to be, whom man encounters even when he is not being just (or unjust) in the narrow sense? We can answer this question in two ways.

Firstly, the partner can be understood as the community, the "social whole." Obviously I am concerned with the common good not only when I keep or break the civil law, when I pay my taxes or go to the polls; the common weal is also involved if I am disorderly or indolent in a seemingly private capacity. The common good requires every individual to be good. "The good of any virtue, whether such virtue direct man in relation to himself, or in relation to certain other individual persons, is referable to the common good, to which justice directs so that all acts of virtue can pertain to justice." [21] And, inversely, every sin can in a certain sense be called an "injustice." [22] This is clearly a much broader notion of justice; and for this reason, justice, as a cardinal virtue, cannot be placed on a [23] rank of equality with "fortitude" and "temperance." Thus, Thomas speaks of "legal" or even "general" justice (*iustitia legalis*, [24] *iustitia generalis*) [25] wherein "all virtue is encompassed," which itself is "the most perfect virtue." [26] And Aristotle found words of poetry for it in the *Nicomachean Ethics*: "The evening star nor the morning star is as glorious" as justice. [27]

Secondly, to say "every moral act has the structure of justice" can also mean that whoever does good or evil stands in relation to God as His "partner," to whom he is giving or withholding His due. "It belongs to general justice (*iustitia generalis*) to do good in relation to the community or in relation to God." [28] So while a man obeys or breaks commandments, he is not dealing with "objective legality" but, rather, with a personal lawgiver, with "some other person."

Nevertheless, the obligation that is to be fulfilled within the scope of justice is utterly distinct from the obligation the man of fortitude or the man of temperance is under—not only in substance but also in structure; not only in the *What* but also in the *How*. The distinction is this: We are able to judge from external appearances what is "objectively" just or unjust, but it does not make any sense to ask what is "objectively" brave and cowardly, temperate and intemperate.

Justice is realized above all in an external act; "in the realm of what is just or unjust, what man does externally is the main point at issue."[29] On the other hand, in the field of fortitude and temperance man's inner state has primarily to be considered and only then, secondarily, his external act. I cannot simply consider a person's act, and on that basis decide whether he is brave, cowardly, temperate, or dissolute; I would have to know more of the person, I would have to know what his disposition is. The justice of an act, on the other hand, can be judged even from the outside, by an impartial third party. How much wine should I drink without violating the virtue of temperance? No stranger could determine that. But, how much do I owe the innkeeper? That can be "objectively" verified by anyone.

This peculiarity of justice, however, that it should first and foremost be realized in an external act (arising, as it does, from my discharging my obligations—whether I do so readily or not, whether I am in need or not, whether my creditor is rich or poor; Kant says: "The other person may be in need or not, he may be in distress or not; but if it is a question of his right, then I am obliged to satisfy it")[30]—this distinguishing mark of justice bears the closest possible relation to the fact that it has, essentially, to do with the "other person." "The other person" is not affected by my subjective disposition, by what I intend, think, feel, or will, but only by what I do. Only by an external act will the other receive what is *his*, his due. "Men are ordained to one another by outward acts, *per exteriores actus*, whereby men live in communion with one another." That is a sentence from the *Summa Theologica*.[31] It is also the reason why, so Thomas says, in the realm of justice good and evil are judged purely on the basis of the deed itself, regardless of the inner disposition of the doer; the point is not how the deed accords with the doer, but rather how it affects "the other person."[32]

The reverse of this statement is also valid. Not only is the act of justice an external act, but every external act belongs to the field of justice. Whatever external act a person performs, it is either just or unjust.

Of course, this does *not* imply that there are no external acts of fortitude, temperance, wantonness as well. Nevertheless, Thomas does maintain the proposition: "*Circa actiones est iustitia*";[33] in any outward act, justice or injustice comes into play. He gives an example: "When through anger one man strikes another, justice is destroyed in the undue blow; while gentleness (*mansuetudo*) is destroyed in the immoderate anger."[34] Such a case of coming to blows and of injured "gentleness" may not seem particularly relevant, but the thesis naturally extends much further. It also implies, for example, that the whole field of sexual aberration, not adultery and rape only, contains an element of injustice. We are not used to perceiving or considering this point. We are apt to concentrate almost exclusively on the subjective significance of dissoluteness as it affects the one who performs the act; whereas it usually escapes us that it is the order of our communal life, and the realization of the common good, which are equally affected, and the more dangerously so the more "external" is the act in question.[35]

Thomas de Vio, also called Cajetan, the commentator of the *Summa Theologica*, formulates a possible objection to this idea in his commentary.[36] He says that an act can be considered from three different points of view, and the *Summa Theologica* names all three of them: the act can be treated in its relationship and fittingness (*commensuratio*) to the one performing it; in its relationship and fittingness to the other person; and thirdly, it can be regarded in itself. Now this is the objection:

Does not Thomas fuse the second and third considerations of an act and confuse the one with the other? Cajetan replies, interpreting Thomas: *Hoc non te moveat*—Don't let this trouble you; if "act" means the same as "external act," then it is related to the other person *of itself*, by the very fact that it is an external act. Consequently, it amounts to the same to say "the act regarded in itself" and "the act regarded in its relation to the other person."

To sum up: *Every* external act is of social consequence. We do not speak without being heard; we do not make use of a thing without using our own or another's property. It is justice, however, that distinguishes what is one's own from that which belongs to another. Whoever teaches is not merely concerned with true and false, above all not with a "private" view of what is true, nor with "personal" opinions. He is quite as concerned with the just or unjust. To teach untruth is not only wrong but unjust as well. All Ten Commandments are *praecepta justitiae*.[38] The whole field of the *vita activa*, also called the *vita civilis* by Thomas—"all of which is defined with reference to our relations with other people"[39]—is the field of justice.

If it is possible to designate the "just thing" apart from the inner condition of the one who performs it, is it perhaps possible, too, to think that a person can *do* the "just thing" without *being* just? In the realm of justice there is actually something approaching a separation of deed and intention. In his treatise on law Thomas says: "The mode of doing acts of justice, which falls under the precept, is that they be done in accordance with right; but not that they be done from the habit of justice"[40]—a formula that is very sober and realistic, it is true, but pretty pointed as well. It states that there is no need for a man to *be* just in order that he may *do* "the just thing." Whence it also follows that a person can *do* something unjust without *being* unjust. And this is possible because there is something "objectively" unjust, whereas it is meaningless to speak of something "objectively" cowardly or patient.

Thus, if a soldier withdraws from a dangerous assignment because he has misunderstood an order,[41] he does not thereby commit an act of cowardice. However, if anyone takes as his own something belonging to another—because he too has misunderstood—he is performing an unjust act, because something is taken from that other person which, in fact, belongs to him. Yet he is not therefore unjust. Once again, this would be quite inconceivable with reference to the other virtues. Whoever behaves himself in an unruly manner, whoever does "something unruly," *is* unruly—at least at that moment. But whoever, carried away by some passion, injures another, commits an unrighteous act, does something unjust, it is true. Nonetheless, he is not necessarily unjust for this reason.[42]

An aside: Should not all this be of some significance for the realm of political discourse, which is of course concerned with what is just and unjust? Does it not imply, for example, that it may be quite possible and logical to reject a certain political objective as "objectively unjust"—and even to combat it with intensity—*without* at the same time bringing the moral integrity of one's opponent into the discussion?

Our present theme, however, is justice as a *virtue*. Now it undoubtedly does pertain to a man's righteousness not only to do the "just thing" but also *to be* just as well. Thomas quotes the *Nicomachean Ethics*:[43] It is an easy matter to do what the just man does; it is difficult, however, for one who does not possess justice to do the just thing *in the way* the just man does it. And he adds: "That is, with promptitude and pleasure."[44] Wherever justice in the full sense is done, the external act is an expression of an inner assent: the other is acknowledged and confirmed in what is due to him. But what *is* due to him cannot be decided from the subjective, inner disposition of the one bound by the obligation. What is due to a person, what is an obligation, can and must be ascertained *objectively*.

"The mean of justice consists in a certain proportion of equality between the external thing and the external person."[45]

3. The Rank of Justice

WHEN THE QUESTION of the rank of a virtue—its place in the scale of eminence among the virtues—is raised in traditional moral teaching, this is not just a whimsical game played with allegorical figures of speech. It is, rather, a very precise delineation of the image of the good man. The question signifies: What makes man fundamentally good and righteous? Understood in this way, the question as to the supreme virtue is usually answered in accordance with the virtue most highly esteemed at a particular period, such as "decency," or "self-control," or "imperturbability," or "courage."

Now traditional teaching says that man reveals his true being in its greatest purity when he is just; justice is the highest of the three moral (in the strict sense) virtues: justice, fortitude, and temperance. The good man is above all the just man. On this point [1] Cicero is cited in the *Summa Theologica*: "Good men are so called chiefly from their justice," "the luster of virtue appears above all in justice." [2] Like the outer porch to the temple, this pre-Christian wisdom is in harmony with Christian doctrine, for Holy Scripture speaks more than eight hundred times of "justice" and "the just man," by which it means no less than "the good, the holy man."

It seems that this insight into the rank of justice is gradually becoming more generally recognized in our time. First, the image of the good man had been modeled after a rather bourgeois concept of "morality," and later after an isolated ideal of "the heroic"; and we have learned that injustice corrupts the fruits of fortitude and that "fortitude without justice is a source (*iniquitatis materia*) of evil."[3] So it is once more possible for us to see that justice, of all the human, natural virtues, is literally the fundamental virtue.

This rank of justice can be established in many ways.

Firstly: Thomas says justice claims a higher rank because it not only orders man in himself but also the life of men together. Justice reaches out beyond the individual subject, because in a certain sense it is itself the *bonum alterius*, the "good of another." The as it were concrete efficacy of good is revealed in a higher manner in justice. For it is in the nature of good to be "*diffusivum sui*," not to be limited to its place of origin but to pour itself out, to work outside itself, to be shared with others, to shine forth. "A thing is more eminently good the more fully and widely it radiates its goodness."[4] "For as that man is most utterly evil who allows his wickedness to hold sway not only over himself but over his friends as well; so is that man most utterly good who not only uses his goodness for himself but for others, too."[5] Now this applies to justice in a higher degree than to the virtues of fortitude and temperance.

Secondly: not only do the object and material of justice (*objectum sine materia*)[6] establish its higher rank, but the *subject* does so, too. Exactly how is the subject of justice to be distinguished from the subject of the other virtues? Is not the subject always man himself, the human person? It is not easy to arrive at an interpretation which makes it clear why St. Thomas is so emphatic on this point.

The human person is naturally the subject of all moral attitudes and decisions. Yet this subject is not a simple, homogeneous reality; above all else it is an entity composed of body and soul. Various virtues can be thought of only because man is a *corporeal* being. A pure spirit cannot be chaste (in the sense of *temperantia*); and such a being has just as little need to moderate the stirring of anger or even to suppress fear. Man, on the other hand, who strives mightily to realize courage and temperance, is beset with the claims of the body; he is the subject of fortitude and temperance in so far as he has bodily existence. But this does not hold true of justice. The demands of justice beset man at his spiritual core. Man is the subject of justice to the extent that he is a spiritual being. Now inasmuch as the power immediately supporting the act of justice is a spiritual desire; "inasmuch as justice," Thomas says, "is in the more excellent part of the soul",[7] inasmuch as the demand on man that he be just is directed at the innermost kernel of his spiritual will, justice holds the foremost rank above all the other moral virtues.

The case is conceivable in which a man has so succeeded, by unceasing *askesis*, in his efforts to create order within himself, that his senses no longer disturb the working of his spiritual soul. What is left for him to do? Well, now, at last, he could achieve what up till now he was prevented from doing, something that he could never realize in its essence: good itself, properly human good. But what is that? Simply this: that man attains to his true treasure and proper realization of himself when he sees the truth and "does the truth." "The good of man, insofar as he is man, consists in his reason's being perfected in the knowledge of truth and his subordinated appetitive powers' being ruled according to the directions of reason."[8] Behind this statement of St. Thomas's stands the thought that in the vision of truth, in contemplation, man attains his proper fulfillment and also the full realization of "human good." But just where does moral virtue find its place within this scheme? Above all, what is the connection between justice and "man's good," which is "the good of reason" or, simply, truth? This is the answer Thomas gives: The good of reason shines more brightly in justice than in any of the other moral virtues; justice is closer to reason.[9] Indeed, the good of reason consists in justice as its proper effect (*sicut in proprio effectu*).[10]

In his treatise on the virtue of fortitude St. Thomas raises the question as to whether or not fortitude is the highest of the cardinal virtues. Once more the reply sets out from the notion of "man's good" (*bonum hominis*); and then, working from this idea, which implies "the good of reason," truth, he formulates the order of the virtues: "Prudence has the good essentially. Justice effects this good; whereas the other virtues . . ."[11] But here it is impossible to suppress the following objection: Is not an act of fortitude or restraint of desire a "realization of the good," too? This objection, however, needs to be clarified. The meaning of the term "act of fortitude" is rather complex. The bravery of an act—for example, if someone risks his life for the community—is a purely internal process, the mastery of fear and of the natural impulse to live. But, on the other hand, the external act of risking one's life, insofar as this is an obligation to the community, is an act of justice. More exactly, then, the objection is this: Is not the restraining of fear and desire, as in courage and temperance, likewise "doing good"? On that score Thomas in fact gives the answer: No! In considering the cardinal virtues, it is only through prudence and justice that man is simply and directly (*simpliciter*) directed toward the good.[12] And for that reason he awards them precedence. But what of fortitude and temperance? The statement our objection interrupted goes on to give the answer: "Whereas the other virtues safeguard this good, inasmuch as they moderate the passions lest they do lead man away from reason's good."[13] But how is this to be understood? To exercise restraint and moderation, to overcome fear of death, is not yet "doing good." These are not properly realizations of the human good. What are they, then? They create the basis—indeed the indispensable basis—for the proper realization of the good.

Thorough confirmation and corroboration of this surprising statement comes from the experience of the great ascetics.

Their experience indicates that the real testing of, as well as the most serious threat to, the inner man, begins only after that basis has been established.

Once more: "Now to be a thing essentially ranks before effecting it, and the latter ranks before safeguarding it by removing obstacles thereto; wherefore amongst the cardinal virtues prudence ranks first, justice second, fortitude third, temperance fourth."[14] We now see clearly why Thomas can say that justice not only has its seat in the will, that is, in the power that is formally directed toward the realization of good, but also that through justice the will is applied to its proper act.[15] *Iustitia est humanum bonum*—Justice is the human good.[16] This conception of the rank which justice occupies can be assessed as a permanent element in the traditional wisdom of the West, quite apart from Thomas. We find a formulation of this very view in the most extreme Platonic wing of that tradition, in Plotinus: Justice simply means "doing one's own work" and "fulfilling one's own task." [17]

The rank of justice is also asserted negatively. "Among all the moral virtues it is justice wherein the use of right reason appears chiefly . . . hence the undue (*indebitus*) use of reason appears chiefly in the vices opposed to justice."[18] The worst disruption of order in the field of things naturally human, that is, the true perversion of "human good," bears the name "injustice."

It is therefore of considerable importance that man prepare himself to encounter historical realizations of evil in which a high degree of "morality" is joined with a considerable measure of "heroism," but which nonetheless remain thoroughly and unsurpassingly inhuman and evil, because at the same time they embody uttermost injustice. We would do well to bear in mind that the uttermost perversion of mankind lies not in excess, which can be easily read in man's bearing and behavior, but in injustice, which, being essentially of the spirit, is not so readily distinguishable. We ought to be prepared to find that the most powerful embodiment of evil in human history, the Antichrist, might well appear in the guise of a great ascetic. This is, in fact, the almost unanimous lesson of historical thinking in the West.[19] Whoever does not understand that it is injustice which is natural man's worst destroyer, and the reason why, will be thrown into overwhelming confusion by the experiences announced in such visions. Above all, he will be powerless to recognize the historical heralds of the abyss. For, even while he watches out in the wrong direction, the forces of destruction will establish their mastery right before his very eyes.

4. The Three Basic Forms of Justice

WHEN MAY JUSTICE be said to prevail in a nation? For the place of justice is in communal life; in an inquiry concerning the realization of justice, we have to direct our attention to the life of the community—to the family, the industrial organization, to the nation organized as a state. One might almost say that the subject of justice is the "community," although of course it is only the person, and, therefore, the individual, who can be just in the strict sense of the word. But to repeat our question: When may justice be said to prevail in a community?

Plutarch, Diogenes Laertius, Stobaeus, have given answers in the form of maxims ascribed to the "Seven Sages." Their replies demonstrate that our question has always been a subject of philosophic speculation. The almost incredible timeliness of their answers proves how very little the passing of time affects this particular field. Thales (of whom Diogenes Laertius reports several very pointed maxims) gives this reply to the question about the strangest thing he had seen in his life: "A tyrant who has grown old."[1] The statesman Thales says: "If there is neither excessive wealth nor immoderate poverty in a nation, then justice may be said to prevail."[2] Bias (to whom is ascribed a thoughtful saying, also quoted by Thomas,[3] of but three words: ἀρχὴ ἄνδρα δείξει—Mastery reveals the man)[4] gives this answer: "When everyone in the state fears the laws as he would fear a tyrant."[5] Solon replies with a well-aimed remark: "Justice rules whenever a criminal is accused and judged in the same way by all those he has *not* injured as he would be by the person to whom he has done some injury."[6] This means that the true character of a criminal wrong is not so much the loss of some possession, the injury to health or life, but, rather, the implicit threat to the entire order of community life, affecting every member. Once this is recognized by everyone, justice can be said to prevail in that state. A series of noteworthy maxims of the Spartan Cheilon have also been handed down to us by Diogenes Laertius. Here is just one example: Three things are surpassingly difficult: keeping a secret, accepting an injustice, making good use of one's leisure.[7] To the question about the just state, Cheilon answers that it is realized whenever the citizen habitually pays most attention to the laws and least to the orators.[8] Pittakos, himself a ruler in his own city, Mytilene, touches in his answer upon the form of government. He says that if it is not possible for the wicked to rule in a *polis*, and if it is likewise not possible for the good to be excluded from ruling, then justice is a reality.[9]

Anyone can see that these replies are not so much a matter of stating formal definitions, rather, of giving some characterizations that have been arrived at empirically, that is, of the precipitate of experience.

St. Thomas's answer might have run like this: Justice rules in a community or state whenever the three basic relations, the three fundamental structures of communal life, are disposed in their proper order: firstly, the relations of individuals to one another (*ordo partium ad partes*); secondly, the relations of the social whole to individuals (*ordo totius ad partes*); thirdly, the relations of individuals to the social whole (*ordo partium ad totum*). These three basic relationships correspond to the three basic forms of justice: reciprocal, or mutually exchanged justice (*iustitia commutativa*), which orders the relation of individual to individual partner; ministering justice (*iustitia distributiva*), which brings order to the relations between the community as such and the individuals who are its members; legal or general justice (*iustitia legalis, iustitia generalis*), which orders the members' relations to the social whole.

The hallmark of all three basic forms of justice is some kind of *indebtedness*, different in character in each case. The obligation to pay the tax collector is different in kind from that of settling my book dealer's account. And the legal protection the state owes the individual is due to me, in principle, in quite a different fashion from that in which my neighbor owes me the return of a loan.

Moreover, a different *subject* is involved in each of these three fundamental forms. To say that commutative justice orders the relations between one individual and another is quite obviously an inadequate formulation. Evidently it is not justice that orders. It is the just man, it is *man* who orders. In the last analysis it is man, and hence the individual person, who supports and realizes all three fundamental forms of justice. Yet the individual is implicated in three different ways. The individual as associate of other individuals sustains commutative justice, whereas the subject of legal justice is, to be sure, once again the individual, but now as the associate of the species, as it were, as a member of the community, as a "subject." So, too, the "social whole" cannot in any concrete sense make distributive justice a reality; again it is rather the individual man—if not the king, then the dictator, the chief of state, the civil servant or even, in a consistent democracy, the individual, insofar as he has a determining role in administering the common good.

One is tempted to give a diagram of these structures, though such a sketch would necessarily be not only inexact but in many details plainly inadequate. Yet inasmuch as that inescapable inadequacy brings into clear focus the necessity for corrections in what has already been said, it will not be wasted effort to give some consideration to a diagram.* And in trying to determine that inadequacy the reader will find that he is personally participating in the present discussion. He will find himself drawn into a controversial discussion and compelled to give a clear-cut interpretation of social reality, which means human reality. In what respect, then, is the schema wrong?

Thomas would see the inaccuracy above all in that the individual and the social whole are represented as separate, sharply distinguished realities, whereas in actual fact the individual who "confronts" the social whole is at the same time included in it as a member. Thomas would always insist that in actual fact individual persons, *personae privatae,*[10] have a reality, an ontological status of their own, and cannot be simply reduced to the reality of the social whole. The human community, the state, Thomas says, is so constructed that the deeds and works of the individual are not of necessity the deeds and works of the whole; and similarly a functioning of the whole as such is possible that is not identical with the functioning of the individual member.[11]

It may be objected that these are abstract speculations. But in order to arrive, for instance, at a sound judgment on the question of collective guilt, we have to go back to this ultimate foundation.

A consistent individualism would raise a totally different objection to our diagram—because its premise is a different interpretation of basic human relations. The individualist's criticism would be that there are in reality only individuals, and that, when an individual confronts the social totality, *one* individual confronts *many* individuals For him the social whole is not a reality of a special order. Therefore he admits of only one single type of justice—commutative justice—because individuals always have to do with other individuals. Every

* See the diagram on p. 113.

phase of man's communal life, in the family as well as in the state, is a compromise between the interests of individuals with equal rights.

A third—the collectivist—interpretation is more immediately timely. It predicates that there is no such thing as an individual capable of entering into relationships in his own right. Above all, no *private* relations between individuals exist. Man's life has a totally public character because the individual is adequately defined only through his membership in the social whole, which is the only reality. Of course no social theory can alter the fact that individuals are actually in relation with each other. Even in the most totalitarian state, I address actual men and hence individuals whenever I speak. However, all such relations can at any moment be interpreted as "official," if they have not been official in the first place. Suddenly I find myself no longer associating with "my" friend, "my" wife, "my" father, but with a co-functionary in the state cause, that is, with a state functionary. As a result, all human relationships are simultaneously subordinated to the yardstick of fulfilling a function, and may abruptly cease to exist when I do not conform to the stipulated norm. Appalling examples of this type are part and parcel of contemporary experience. Needless to say, from this point of view the concept of commutative justice becomes meaningless;[12] as, equally, the concept of distributive justice, which proclaims that an individual has rights not only in his relations with other individuals but with the social whole as well. And even the seemingly unaffected concept of *iustitia legalis*, which formulates the individual's obligation toward the functions of the state, has in the last analysis become unthinkable. The notion of justice has ceased to be applicable in any sense whatsoever.

The end result of this reasoning seems decidedly noteworthy. It becomes evident that the very essence of justice is threatened the moment the serious claim is made that these three fundamental structures of the communal life (structures that are independent of each other), and hence the three basic forms of justice, simply do not exist. It seems that at least such a threefold structure is required to do justice to the extremely complex reality contained in the all-too-glibly treated twin concepts "individual and society." But of course the decisive factor is not the purely intellectual admission of conceptual distinctions. The important thing, rather, is that justice prevail and become a reality, in its threefold form.

5. Recompense and Restitution

COMPENSATORY or commutative justice is, as it were, the classic form of justice, for several reasons. First of all, in the relations between individuals, every partner actually confronts an "other person" quite independent of himself; the "*ad alterum*" is a fully realized fact. In the other two fundamental relations, however, the individual does not properly "confront" the "we" (those with whom he is in contact and who are associated with him) as another separate person. Then, too, the partner's equal rights are unreservedly realized only in the situation of commutative justice. But here a second element in the true concept of justice is suggested: "Justice is simply (*simpliciter*) between those who are simply equal, but where there is no absolute equality between them, neither is there absolute justice."[1]

One consequence of this is that this kind of justice is not thinkable in the relations between God and man. "Commutative justice, strictly so-called, cannot be said of God because it would presuppose an equality between God, who gives, and the creature, who receives."[2]

In the manner of commutative justice that individual is just who gives the other person, the unrelated individual, the stranger, what is his due—neither less nor more. To be sure, *commutatio* (changing hands, the transfer of a thing from one person to another)[3] also applies in the making of a gift. Yet to give a present is not an act of justice because the thing given is in no sense owed, is not a *debitum*.[4] On this score, Thomas insists most energetically that justice should not go beyond what is owed. This is not, I think, mere pedantry. Still less is it a matter of niggardly minimalism. Rather it means, soberly and without romantic illusion: the ideal image of *iustitia commutativa* demands that a man be able to acknowledge the rights particularly of the stranger, whether he be in fact unrelated, or felt to be alien, perhaps because he suddenly appears as "competitor," threatening one's own interests, a person whose affairs are "none of my business," whom I "don't care for," to whom I would not dream of making a gift; against whom, rather, I have to hold my ground and assert myself. To this very stranger I have to give his due, neither more nor less: this is justice.

The charge of minimalistic niggardliness could also be raised against contractual agreements, the established form of balancing interests, which is why *iustitia commutativa* has also been called "contract justice." There are persons and movements who, in an unrealistic overvaluation of "community" ideals, regard the balancing of interests by contract as an inferior form of regulating human relationships, since they are based only on the "cold" calculation of one's own advantage.[5]

It is true that the partners to a contract are "interested parties." The very meaning of a contract is, indeed, to mark the limits of each party's rights and to guarantee one party's claim to a certain return as much as the other's obligation to make that return. If love says: "Whatever belongs to me should belong to the one I love, too," justice proclaims: "To each his own." Which means that what is yours is yours, and what is mine is mine. In relations built on love, that is, in relations truly "shared" between man and man, there is no call for either contract or, in the strict sense, for justice.

Countering the romantic overvaluation of a special form of communal life, we have to bear in mind that, if the contract represents a balancing of interests, it also represents a form of mutual understanding. We perceive only one part of the real-

ity if we consider nothing but the self-assertion of the party to
a contract. The other part, at least where a just and equitable
contract is concerned (which is here taken for granted—
though a just contract is not a declaration of love, but remains
a method of balancing interests), is the mutual acknowledgment of the parties. A contract implies a genuine obligation
and tie, as well as an expressly affirmed restriction of one's
own interest by the other party's interest. The reality of a
contractual balance of interests includes the faithful fulfillment
of the contract. It involves the acknowledgment of the principle of equality between service and counter-service. To sum
up: a contract is an instrument not of self-assertion only, but
also of rendering the "other" his due. However true it may be
that man's communal life cannot attain its fullest realization
through *iustitia commutativa* alone, it is no less true that in its
ideal image the irreducible core of social relations finds expression, that is the foundation which even the higher and richer
forms of mutual agreement require.

It is not easy to exhaust the implications of the proposition
in the *Summa Theologica* which says: The act of justice
which orders the association of individuals with one another[6] is
restitutio, recompense, restoration. A French translation tends
to weaken what Thomas has said and makes an interpretative
insertion to the effect that it is not a question of *the* act of
commutative justice but of its principal act (*acte premier*).[7]
However, the sense of even this interpretation is that in the
field of *iustitia commutativa* "restitution" occupies a unique
place. As a matter of fact there is nothing about any other act
in Thomas.

What, then, is *restitutio?* Thomas himself gives the answer.
"It is seemingly the same as once more (*iterato*) to re-instate a
person in the possession or dominion of his thing."[8] It is, then, a
re-storation, a *re*-compense, a *re*-turning. What are we to make
of these reiterations? I think we would lose insight into the

meaning hidden here if we were to reduce *restitutio* simply to its present significance of restitution, that is, of returning another person's property and making reparation for some illegally wrought injury.[9] Rather, we are here concerned with "surprise" formulations that point to some unexpressed thought which is self-evident to Thomas but not to us. A key to what is meant here can be found in such a familiar phrase as: "To give to each his own." There is something very much to the point in Schopenhauer's objection: "If it is his own, there is no need to *give* it to him."[10] A condition of justice is the startling fact that a man may *not* have what is nonetheless "his own"—as the very concept of "something due a person" implies. Consequently, the recognition of the *suum* can rightly be called re-storation, a re-stitution, re-compense, re-instatement to an original right. And this does not apply only to cases like theft, fraud, and robbery (Thomas speaks of *commutationes involuntariae*, changes in original ownership which take place against the will of one of the partners).[11] It is not only in this area that it is meaningful to speak of *restitutio*; wherever one man owes another something (even in such voluntary obligations as buying, renting, or borrowing)[12] or wherever due respect is shown and due thanks are expressed, to give what is due is always "restitution."

The state of equilibrium that properly corresponds to man's essence, to his original, "paradisiac" state, is constantly thrown out of balance, and has constantly to be "restored" through an act of justice. Nor must the disturbance be necessarily understood as injustice, though the fact that the act of justice is called *restitutio* presupposes that injustice is the prevalent condition in a world dominated by opposing interests, the struggle for power, and hunger. To bring solace and order into the conflict of contending interests which by their nature are legitimate opposites and not easily reconcilable, to impose on them, as it were, a posterior order, is the office and task of commutative justice. The establishment of equity has as its premise that there is no natural equality, or that it exists not yet, or no longer. That man, especially, is just who does not become inured and hardened to disorder, not even to a disorder he may have originated himself at first impulse (to become a man means learning to be unjust, says Goethe). The just man recognizes when wrong has been done, admits his own injustice, and endeavors to eradicate it. Who would deny that we touch here the sore spot in all reciprocal relationships, and that the basic way to realize commutative justice does in fact have the character of restitution?

Yet, as has already been said, we need not turn our attention only to compensation for injustice. Man's every act "disturbs" the stable equilibrium, since every act turns the doer into either a debtor or a creditor. And since men are constantly becoming indebted to one another, the demand is constantly raised to pay that debt by an act of "restitution." Therefore, the equality that characterizes justice cannot be finally and definitely established at any one time, it cannot be arrested. It must, rather, be constantly re-established, "restored anew" (*iterato*). It has to be "reinstated." The "return to equilibrium," which, Thomas says, occurs in *restitutio*,[13] is an unending task. This means that the dynamic character of man's communal life finds its image within the very structure of every act of justice. If the basic act of commutative justice is called "*restitution*," the very word implies that it is never possible for men to realize an ideal and definitive condition. What it means is, rather, that the fundamental condition of man and his world is provisory, temporary, nondefinitive, tentative, as is proved by the "patchwork" character of all historical activity, and that, consequently, any claim to erect a definitive and unalterable order in the world must of necessity lead to something inhuman.

6. Distributive Justice

WHOEVER speaks of distributive justice has to speak of exercise of power. What is under discussion is the right order in the relation between those who have power and those who are entrusted or delivered to this power. That is why a discussion of *iustitia distributiva* is the very center of the theory of justice.

Let us recall the characteristic structure of distributive justice by reminding ourselves that an individual man is not confronted with another individual only, nor even with many individuals. He is confronted by the social whole. It becomes clear at once that the two partners are not of equal rank, not only because many are more than one, but also because the common weal belongs to another and higher order than the good of the individual.[1] Nevertheless, it is the individual who is the partner with the claim in this relationship. He is the one to whom something is due. This means that, on the other hand, the social whole is the partner bound by an obligation. The social whole ranks higher than the individual, and yet it is bound by an obligation. We have already said that this concept cannot be realized by a consistent individualism, and certainly not by collectivism.

Hence the claim expressed in the ideal image of *iustitia distributiva* is formally directed toward the social whole, the governor, the ruler, the lawgiver. Man, as administrator of the common weal, is brought to account and is obliged to give the individual members of the whole their due. The ideal image of distributive justice, however, does not authorize individuals to determine and assert on their own initiative what is due to them on the part of the social whole. But though they are not so authorized, this does not mean that such a premise would be impossible and intrinsically counter to justice. Rather, where justice is under discussion, whenever it is said, "Thou shalt be just," the reference is not to the claimant, but to the one who has to grant the due. In the case of *iustitia distributiva* this means: the claim and appeal is directed to man in so far as he represents the social whole. The fact that at first thought we no longer consider the administrator of the common weal as a person, that we have ceased to visualize him as an individual open to personal approach and consider him as a faceless mechanism, shows the dangerous extent to which we are already conditioned by collectivist thinking.

One more point has to be considered in order to make clear the structure of distributive justice. There is an obligation due to the individual in his relation toward the social whole that is in principle different from his due as creditor toward debtor in a situation of commutative justice. What belongs to him and the way it belongs to him are quite different. In the case of commutative justice, a creditor has the right to receive the equivalent of a service he has rendered or reparation for a loss he has sustained. It is his due as something belonging to him exclusively as an individual. But what is the individual's due in the case of *iustitia distributiva*? Nothing belongs to him as exclusively his, *non id quod est proprium*; all that belongs to him is a share in something common to everyone, *id quod est commune*.[2] In this instance the individual is not an independent, separate party to a contract with claims equal to those of his partner, as in *iustitia commutativa*. He is faced with a partner of higher rank, of which he himself is a part. "Distributive justice . . . distributes common goods proportionately."[3] "There are two kinds of justice: the one consists in mutual giving and receiving . . . the other consists in distribution, *in distribuendo*, and is called distributive justice; whereby a ruler or steward gives to each what his rank deserves." [4]

Several tangible consequences follow from this.

Firstly: In the situation of commutative justice, the due can be as surely calculated and determined by the party entitled to it as by the party obligated to pay it—or even by an impartial third party. That is *not* possible in the case of *iustitia distributiva*. Determining what is the due of any one person can only be effected from the position and viewpoint of the one responsible for the common weal, for the very reason that a due and fitting share in the common good is involved. In both cases an obligation is established. But in the one case the obligation is paid, in the other case it is allotted. If I sell my house, I can leave the price due to me to be ascertained by a third party, or I can bargain with the buyer, or I can simply demand it. If, however, following the practice of equitable sharing of burdens, some compensation is due me from the state to cover damage to my house during wartime, I cannot determine independently what is rightfully mine. Only the responsible guardian of the common weal can establish what is due to me, as he is concerned with the *bonum commune*.

Secondly: In the case of *iustitia distributiva* justice and equity cannot be achieved by consideration of the actual value only. In commutative justice such an approach is both possible and meaningful. A just price can be determined without reference to the person of the buyer or seller, simply by taking into consideration the market value of the object that is to be sold. In this case justice and equity consist in the *aequalitas rei ad rem*, as Thomas formulates it.[5] In the relation between the social whole and individuals, on the contrary, what is just is determined as "whatever corresponds to the thing's proportion to the person."[6] That means that the one who administers the common good may not consider the object of the obligation alone. Instead, he has to keep the subjects of the obligation in view as well. He must consider the individuals with whom he has to deal. Thus, in the case of indemnity for war damage, the true value of the damage is not the only thing to be considered. Justice might demand the taking into account of such factors as whether or not the damage has completely impoverished the person, whether or not he had already made any other great sacrifice for the social whole (as in the case of a refugee or a battle casualty).

Thus, the compromise that has to be effected [7] both in distributive justice and in commutative justice has a quite distinct character in each instance. In the first case it is a "proportional" equality (*aequalitas proportionis*), in the other a purely numerical, "quantitative" equality (*aequalitas quantitatis*). In the same place in his commentary on the *Nicomachean Ethics*,[8] again following Aristotle,[9] Thomas has pointed out that this distinction is the same as the difference between a geometric and an arithmetic proportion.

The reader may possibly get the impression that what has been said of distributive justice up to this point has a distinctly "totalitarian" tinge. It is part and parcel of the intellectual and political atmosphere of the day that this should be an almost compulsive reaction. The idea that there is in distributive justice a single authority that administers the common good and that is able, by virtue of its own rights, to decide what and how much is due to me, is almost inevitably linked with that other idea of enslaving the individual and encroaching upon his rights. And at the same time a picture of "democracy" looms up alongside it as the (supposedly) only remaining alternative, which leaves no room for genuine authority and thus again veers toward despotism or has it close in its wake. In view of this literally fatal choice, it is decisive that we should recognize the ideal image of *iustitia distributiva* and make it a reality. Two things are combined in this image: the affirmation of genuine authority and at the same time the recognition of the individual person to whom his right is absolutely due from the social whole.

It is this very absoluteness, however, which gives rise to the emotional objection. Rationally formulated, it would amount to something like this: You say that in the individual's relationship with the social whole something is due to the individual, but not, as in the case of commutative justice, as an exclusive personal right; rather, it is his share in a property common to all. But are there not things to which I have an irrevocable, a truly absolute claim, even when confronted with the social whole, with the state?

The state, we may note, occupies a unique place in the scale that extends from the individual to the whole of mankind; more than anything else, it represents the "social whole." The idea of the common good is its distinctive attribute. A nation (in the midst of other nations) ordered in a state is the proper, historically concrete image of man's communal life. *Communitas politica est communitas principalissima*—Political community is community in the highest degree.[10] In the fullest sense the state alone incorporates, realizes, and administers the *bonum commune*. That does not mean, however, that the family, the community, free associations, and the Church are not important for the realization of the common good, too. But it means that the harmonizing and integration of nearly all men's functions occurs only in the political community. In the state alone is sovereignty vested and with it the authority and the power to maintain the *bonum commune* in its fullest sense—an authority which includes the full right to impose punishment. "Since the state is a perfect society, the ruler of the state possesses full power of compulsion. Therefore, he can inflict irreparable punishment such as death or mutilation."[11] "On the other hand, the father and the master who preside over the family household, which is an imperfect community, have imperfect coercive power."[12] To sum up, the state is, to a degree encountered in almost no other instance, the representative of the "social whole," of "us."

But to get back to our question. How are we to proclaim the inalienability of the individual's rights vis-à-vis the state if, on the other hand, it is true that in the relationships characteristic of *iustitia distributiva* nothing is due to the individual which is exclusively his? First of all, let us briefly consider the special nature of this kind of obligation. The objection presumably refers first and foremost to the right to life, health, and freedom. In what respect is there a special form of obligation in the relationship between individual and state? In his relation to the state, the individual's right to life and health, for example, is not so exclusively his that the state might not require or curtail it in the interest of the common good. Against any individual, I may in an emergency defend my life, health, freedom, even my property, to the extent of killing the aggressor. Public authority, however, can quite legitimately deprive an individual of his freedom, not only when he has committed a crime, but also when it happens that through no fault of his he has fallen victim to a contagious disease that would endanger the social whole. And the administrator of the *bonum commune* can even make decrees affecting the individual's property under certain conditions.

All this does not in any sense imply that the authority of the state must first "endorse" life, freedom and property for the individual, nor that it can grant them to him. Yet, no matter how the powers of public authority are constituted and limited, this much at all events is clear: in his relationship with public authority, a *suum* belongs to a private person in a fashion quite different from that applying to his relations to another private person. It is this peculiar structure in the actual fabric of communal life that we bring to light when we get to the roots of the distinction between commutative justice and distributive justice.

Is there not, then, something "inalienable," as it were, in the individual's rights over and against the social whole? Yes, there is. Wherein does it manifest itself? It is revealed in the limitations and conditions set for these encroachments of the state's authority: that power can only be wielded "*if* the common good demands it." As a member of the whole, the individual has an inalienable right to expect that the distribution of goods, as well as of burdens, be effected justly (that is, justly in the manner of *iustitia distributiva*). But is there any way to render the individual's inalienable rights secure? Is there any effective way to defend them?

At this point we shall have to speak of another peculiarity of *iustitia distributiva*. We are in the habit of saying that the distinguishing mark of an obligation in the realm of justice is that it is possible to compel its execution. The fulfillment of *iustitia distributiva*, however, cannot be enforced. It is inherent in the concept that no such enforcement should be possible. For who, indeed, is to compel the man in public authority to give the individual what is due to him? Yet it is to him, as the person invested with the state's authority, that distributive justice extends its claims: he is the subject of this particular form of justice. We have here the instance of a person under a definite obligation to grant something that is due to an individual, to give people their "just due," and who yet cannot be compelled to do so. There is no question but that in this instance the inalienability of an individual's rights, which continues to obtain, takes on a very special hue.

If an individual cannot come to some agreement with his neighbor, for instance in the question of settling a debt, both can bring the matter before a third authority, before a court of law. But if a person feels he has not obtained his due from the public authority, there is no "impartial" authority before whom he may bring the matter. But are not "appeal" and "review" possible in the case of an unjust judgment in a court of law? Here we must endeavor to see clearly what this recourse from one authority to the next really means. The highest courts of law, like the lower courts, are organs of but one and the same juridical society. Even the highest tribunal examines nothing but the legal aspects of a case and the application of existing laws. But what if the laws themselves are unjust? What if injustice befalls an individual on the basis of existing laws, simply because he belongs to a certain race, class, or religious community? This would be a case in point. To whom, then, could an "appeal" be addressed? Not to mention situations which do not even allow the opportunity for an objection, as, for instance, in the case of an enemy attack, when of necessity the most far-reaching measures may interfere with private rights.

In view of the objective injustice of certain laws, directives, decrees, and orders, the question naturally arises concerning the rights of resistance and nonobservance, yet never in such a form that the individual affected by those laws and regulations could appear jointly with their author before the tribunal of an independent, superior party equipped with compulsory power. In short, the person invested with the authority of the state, the man who is the subject of *iustitia distributiva*, cannot actually be compelled to the just performance of his office because he himself is at one and the same time guardian and executor of distributive justice. "A ruler is installed for the purpose of guarding justice."[13]"The purpose of power is to realize justice."[14]What if the guardian of justice nevertheless does *not* guard it? Well, then, alas, there is the reign of injustice. And no appeal to any abstract arbiter such as "the conscience of mankind," "the eye of the world," and "the judgment of history" can in any way change it.

Whoever thoroughly examines the structure of *iustitia distributiva* must come to realize very clearly the nature of genuine authority, and to see that no worse or more desperate mishap can be imagined in the world of men than unjust government. And since institutional precautions and controls could entirely prevent the abuse of power only by precluding any form of effective authority, there is nothing and no one that can restrain the man of power from doing injustice—if not his own sense of justice. In the affairs of the world, everything depends on the rulers' being just.

We have already said that the traditional doctrine of justice is concerned not with the claimant but with the man owing a claim. It is not concerned with the declaration of human rights, belonging to men as their legitimate claim. Rather, it is the proclamation and establishment of the obligation to respect rights.[15] We are not saying this at this juncture merely for the sake of moralizing. What we have in mind has quite a different significance. At first glance it seems to be a much more aggressive approach to declare rights than to proclaim and establish duties. In reality, quite the reverse is the case. Is not the declaration of a claim by the one entitled to it more of a defensive gesture? A gesture based on a kind of resignation (perhaps a not unfounded one) to the fact that the men under obligation would not concede what is due unless the claimant backed up his demands by force? Reference to the *obligation* in justice, on the other hand, is not only more audacious, but far more realistic as well—all appearances to the contrary. Reference here, to be sure, is not used as a rhetorical term. It is meant to designate the convincing proof of the ground upon which such an obligation rests, and in particular whatever might serve, in the broadest sense, the realization of justice as a human virtue in the state. This approach, therefore, is far more realistic because in the final reckoning it will only be through justice that each man will be given the share that is his, through the justice of those who can give or deny what is due to men; because merely asserting rights never creates justice; because justice in distribution will be realized only through just government. It is an illusion fostered by our socio-technological thinking to assume that a mere organizational perfection of political life, for instance through built-in automatic controls, might render justice as a virtue obsolete—"the steadfast will (of the individual of course!) to give each man his due."

If, however, it is a Utopian dream to think that just government can exist in the world, if it is a Utopian goal to think that the educative efforts of a people should primarily aim at forming the young generation, especially those called to leadership, into just men—then all hope must indeed be abandoned.

One thing, of course, is indispensable: that a sense of the greatness and dignity of governing and ruling[16] be revived in the mind of the public. This is all the more necessary since the "intellectuals" of the past hundred years have been virtually defined by their ironical treatment of the terms "authority" and "subject," with the result that nowadays these words can hardly be spoken or understood without bias. Individualistic liberalism is in fundamental agreement with orthodox Marxism on this point, namely that there is no "governmental authority" properly so called. For individualism, authority is vested in agreements between individuals which, as a matter of principle, can be canceled at any time; for Marxism, it is the hallmark of those preliminary stages of society which will one day dissolve altogether within a Communist society.[17]

In his *Politics*[18] Aristotle has raised the question whether or not being a good citizen and a good man are one and the same thing. Can a person who is not a good man nonetheless be a good citizen in the *polis*? He leaves the question in abeyance. On the one hand, he says, a state cannot possibly be composed of nothing but excellent men, and nevertheless there are excellent states. On the other hand, there are states (and they are not the just states) wherein a person can be one of the better and more desirable citizens without being a good man.[19] We are struck by the timeliness of this thought. Aristotle adds a thoughtful statement which is of interest to us here. He says: There is, perhaps, *one* citizen who is required to be a good man also (that is, good as man, a man wholly and entirely in order) and that man is the ruler. And on the other hand, the just ruler —according to Bias's maxim that mastery reveals the man—[20] has always been considered as a pre-eminently excellent representative of human virtue, as a man who by the justice of his rule proves that he has resisted those superhuman temptations which assail only men in authority.

In his treatise on political government[21] Thomas asks about the suitable reward a just king can expect to receive, "since the king's duty to seek the people's good may seem too onerous a task, unless something good accrues to him for himself. It is worth contemplating, then, just what kind of suitable reward there is for a good king." Wealth, honor, and renown are mentioned,[22] but all of them put together are considered an inadequate recompense. And when Thomas concludes this magnificent passage with the statement that the just ruler will, "as his reward, be near God and stand at His side inasmuch as he has faithfully exercised the king's divine office over his people,"[23] it means that he apportions to the good ruler an incomparable, almost metaphysical distinction of rank, not by virtue of the religious character of his consecration, but on the grounds of his just rule. This view is further strengthened by the words then added: "Even pagan peoples had some prophetic presentiment of this when they believed the leaders and guardians of the people would be transformed into gods." It is more than arbitrary "poetic" allegory when, in his *Divine Comedy*, Dante sees the just kings in the constellation Aquila, fashioned in the shape of an eagle by the lights of those rulers who had been taken up into heaven.[24]

Such formulations are misunderstood if they are interpreted romantically. They are actually based on a highly realistic insight into the danger that usually threatens the ruler, and into the almost superhuman difficulty involved in making *iustitia distributiva* a reality.

If political life is to regain its dignity, a proper appreciation of the eminence of the ruler's task and of the lofty human qualities required for it must be revived in the mind of the public. This means the very opposite of a totalitarian glorification of power. It implies rather that an arduous and unremitting effort of education should impart to the people an incontrovertible ideal image of the requirements a man must meet if he is to exercise authority. It should, for example, be perfectly clear and self-evident to the simplest kind of thinking that wherever prudence and justice are lacking, there can be no fitness for the proper exercise of power. In Aristotle's *Politics*,[25] as well as in the *Summa Theologica* of Thomas Aquinas,[26] these two cardinal virtues are called the virtues characteristic of sovereigns and rulers. Yet according to the moral doctrine of the West the prudent man is certainly not merely a "tactician" able to steer an affair successfully to its conclusion. Prudence implies the kind of objectivity that lets itself be determined by reality, by insight into the facts. He is prudent who can listen in silence, who can take advice so as to gain a more precise, clear, and complete knowledge of the facts. If such a standard were applied, it would probably mean that even without formally rejecting him—in fact *before* there were any discussion about him—a rash, brash person, motivated by emotion or craving for power, would *eo ipso* be excluded from running for office, as manifestly unfit to realize the justice of rulers, *iustitia distributiva*. For exercising this justice means, on the one hand, taking the common good into consideration and, on the other, respecting at the same time the dignity of the individual and giving him what is his due.

Up to this point we have spoken of the "ruler" or "king" as the administrator of the common good. In respect to contemporary conditions, our terminology, of course, needs to be corrected and made more precise. But even though there is no occasion in this present context to treat the different forms of government in detail, it may still be noted in passing that according to Thomas Aquinas, monarchy is the form of government which of its very nature most readily guarantees sensible administration of the common good. He also says, however, that of all the possible ways in which authority may degenerate, *unjust* monarchy is the worst. "Just as kingly rule is the best, so is the rule of the tyrant the worst."[27] And there is still another astonishing remark of St. Thomas to consider, namely that tyranny arises more easily and frequently from democracy than from the rule of kings.[28]

In a modern democracy, then, who is the subject of *iustitia distributiva*? The chosen representatives and delegates of the people are the direct subjects; indirectly the voters are. In this connection we should remember that voters are hardly ever active directly as single individuals, but are organized into parties which (as suitable machinery for forming opinion) both name the representatives to be elected and formulate their concrete political aims. The distinctive peculiarity of the democratic form of government as compared with monarchy consists above all—apart from the short period for which the delegate is appointed—in the fact that the representative of the social whole is to a much greater extent the representative of particular groups or interests as well. Therefore, if ruling is tantamount to administering the general good of everyone (a notion which is formally denied, for instance, in a concept like the "dictatorship of the proletariat"),[29] then the way in which democracy functions imposes the following tremendous moral burden upon the individuals, voters and delegates alike: the individual is obligated by an ideal image of just distribution without ceasing to be interested in his own particular right. The main problem facing modern party democracy is: How can a party still be impartial? I would not say it is impossible. Indeed, any inconsidered polemic against party politics as such is highly unrealistic and for that reason irresponsible. Yet we must see that a real problem and a very specific danger do exist here—or rather, a task, namely the task of educating men to *iustitia distributiva.*

In this field there are several classic cases of failure. The following example dates from the last years of the Weimar Republic: In one of the great wage disputes of that time, the two parties involved in the dispute appealed to the decision of the federal minister of labor, as a final tribunal. Whereupon this man, who in his role of minister and arbitrator was under a twofold obligation to the *bonum commune,* declared that in this case he was primarily secretary of the trade unions and only secondarily a member of the federal government.[30]

Here the limitations of democracy as a form of government, that is, as a ministering of the common good, come to light. The limit is reached when it can no longer be expected of an individual that he place the *bonum commune* above his own particular interest. It is not possible, I believe, to determine that precise limit once and for all. Historically speaking there is very considerable scope for variation in terms of the level a people's political education has attained. Thus, in one instance democracy as a government actually exercised jointly by everyone in the community does "work"; in another case it does not.[31] Yet it seems that there are certain boundaries beyond which it cannot be expected from human frailty that concern for the welfare of the whole should overrule the individual's immediate concern or the interest of a special group; these boundaries seem to set limits for democracy as well. There can be little doubt, for instance, that in a "first ballot," the average person cannot be expected to answer the question: "Do you want a higher wage, a tax cut, release from the draft, etc., or not?" with the *bonum commune* primarily in view.

Thus, the question: Who actually realizes *iustitia distributiva?* does not always receive a full answer. Thomas says that it is primarily the one who administers the *bonum commune*; but the individual, the "subject" (*subditus*), is also called to the realization of the ideal image of distributive justice; he, too, can be just in the manner of *iustitia distributiva*—indeed, he must be so, if the challenge of the virtue of justice is to be satisfied. Thomas, however, is not speaking here of the individual as participating in the shaping of the common good as voter or delegate; he is thinking of the individual in his capacity as taxpayer, for example, or as the man subject to military service—as "the governed," in brief. But how can the individual, from that point of view, still be considered to be a subject of distributive justice, since he has not the slightest chance of "distributing" anything? Thomas gives the following answer: "The act of distributing the goods of the community belongs to none but those who exercise authority over those goods; and yet distributive justice is also in the subjects (*in subditis*) to whom these goods are distributed, insofar as they are contented by a just distribution."[32] This "contentment on the part of the ruled" should not be interpreted as stolidity. It is part of the act of justice to give one's conscious consent to the just and equitable decrees of a political authority acting in the interest of the common good—and not just lip service, but, rather, a consent that molds the actual attitude and conduct. Through his act of consenting, the "subject" takes part in the ruler's justice.

Such a premise does not exclude a legitimate right to criticism and "opposition." (In fact, Thomas is even of the opinion that laws which do not serve the true common good do not possess any binding power.)[33] It does, however, oppose a biased, negative attitude, illoyal from the very start. Unwarranted criticism and opposition, blind abuse and fault-finding, are acts of injustice, violations of *iustitia distributiva* which alone enables states to exist and function in orderly fashion.

Once again it is clear that we are here touching upon a danger inherent in the democratic form of government. Once more we come to a point which calls for rigorous political self-discipline. We are reminded of the words of Donoso-Cortés, in a parliamentary address of 1850 concerning the European situation: "The evil that confronts our time is that those who are ruled no longer are willing to be ruled."[34] At this juncture the parliamentary record comments: "Laughter." Donoso-Cortés wanted to imply that genuine authority not only requires men fitted for the offices of government, but also presupposes an inner disposition on the part of the governed, a readiness to participate in the just rule by giving their consent to a just administering of the *bonum commune*.

Exactly *what* is distributed in the act of *iustitia distributiva*? We have already quoted the following text from the *Summa Theologica*: "In distributive justice something is given to a private individual insofar as what belongs to the whole is due to the part."[35] This means that the share in the *bonum commune* due to the individual is "distributed" to him.

This is the place, then, to seek a somewhat clearer understanding of the concept of "*bonum commune*." Provisionally, the *bonum commune* might be defined as follows: it is the "social product," the total product of community life. The element of truth in this answer is that individuals do work together in all the group activities and professions within a society and co-operate in the production of something that is quite unique, and perhaps irreducible to organized concepts. The result is that food, clothing, shelter, means of communication, transmission of news, care of the sick, education and schools, along with many other kinds of goods for consumption, are now available for the people, that is, the "social whole." The concept *iustitia distributiva* would mean that all these goods are shared and "distributed" in like manner to all members of the community.

One remark: The concepts of "class," "class dispute," and "class struggle" have their place within this context. There is no compelling reason why any Western theory of society should ignore these notions. For the idea of "class dispute" is not to be considered as purely negative. The implication is rather:[36] if one social segment, that is, a considerable group of the people, considers the prevailing method of sharing the total social product as detrimental to its own legitimate interests and opposes it, therefore, as contrary to the spirit of true communal life, then that social group has become a "class." This attack against the prevailing order generates automatically the resistance of that stratum of the society which is interested in maintaining the *status quo* and will therefore defend it. This defense again leads automatically to the formation of another "class." Class dispute, therefore, is the natural result of the existence of various classes within a society. And it is quite conceivable that there might be a class dispute animated by a desire for justice.[37] A totally different meaning attaches to the term "class struggle" in orthodox Marxism. Here, class struggles strive to annihilate the opposing class and to destroy order in a nation. Fruitful dispute among classes, on the contrary, which aims at the "deproletarianizing of the proletariat," not only does not abolish order in the nation (though it may be in constant danger of deteriorating into class struggle), but actually has that order as its goal.

I said above that provisionally we might try to define the concept *"bonum commune"* as the total social product. Yet this definition is still not quite adequate. First of all, it originates in the mental outlook of our technological age, which tends to see the true end of society in the techniques of production; in view of its origin, such a definition harbors the danger of obscuring the fact that the *bonum commune* extends far beyond the range of material goods produced by mechanical means. There are contributions to the common weal which, though not immediately "useful," are still indispensable —and of very real value, as well. This is no doubt the sense in which St. Thomas's text is to be understood: The perfection of the human community demands that there be men who dedicate themselves to a life of contemplation,[38] a tenet which signifies that the society of men relies for its functioning on a knowledge of the truth, and that nations thrive in proportion to the depth of reality opened up and accessible to them.

It becomes possible at this point to formulate a preliminary definition of the totalitarian labor state. It belongs to the principle of such a state that the common good is equated with "common utility." Its projects for the realization of the *bonum commune* are exclusively concerned with utilitarian ends.

A second objection to the definition: The *bonum commune* is the social product, strikes at a much more basic inadequacy. By virtue of the original and enduring meaning of the term *bonum commune*, it represents *the good* (the very essence of those good things) for the sake of which a community exists, and which it must attain and make a reality if it is to be said that all its potentialities have been brought to fruition. For this very reason it appears impossible to give a truly exhaustive, definitive definition of the *bonum commune*; for no one can state with complete finality what the potentialities of the human community are, what the human community "fundamentally" is. No one can give a truly exhaustive account of what man himself "fundamentally" is, and consequently it is just as impossible to give an exhaustive account of everything contained in man's "good," for the sake of which man exists and which he has to realize in his life if it is to be said of him that all his potentialities have been brought to fruition. This and nothing else is the meaning behind the assertion so stubbornly defended by Socrates: that he did not know what "human virtue" was and that he had still to meet the man who knew better.

If we are thus to understand *bonum commune*, what do we mean when we say that we give a man that share in the common good which is due to him? What does it mean to realize *iustitia distributiva*? It means to let individual members of a nation share in the realization of a *bonum commune* that cannot be definitively delineated in concrete terms. Taking part in the realization of that good in accordance with the measure of *dignitas*, capacity, and ability that is distinctively his, this is the share which "is due to" the individual and which cannot be withheld from him by the person administering the *bonum commune* without violating *iustitia distributiva*, the justice proper to rulers. This suggests a much wider reference, namely, that all the good things bestowed in creation (men's capacities and abilities) belong to the "good of the community," and that *iustitia distributiva* entails the obligation of granting such abilities the protection, support, and fostering they need.

With this it becomes possible to formulate one more essential element of totalitarian government. The person endowed with political power claims to give a comprehensive definition of the tangible content of the *bonum commune*. The fact that a "five-year plan" tries to achieve a higher rate of industrial production or seeks a closer adjustment between supply and demand is not in itself a fatally destructive feature. What is fatally destructive is the elevation of such a "plan" to an exclusive standard to which not only the production of goods is subordinated but also the work at the universities, the creative activity of the artist, and the use of leisure. Thus, everything that cannot be justified by this standard must, for that simple reason, suffer suppression as "socially unimportant" and "undesirable."

It is in the nature of things that a "distributor" should take some thought of the person who receives, but that a "buyer" should consider only the actual objective value of the thing received. Here we are faced, as has already been said, with the main distinction between *iustitia distributiva* and commutative justice. In fulfilling the justice of government the administrator of the *bonum commune* necessarily considers the person and his *dignitas* (dignity can, in this case, signify both a special aptitude for a certain office and "worthiness" [in the proper sense], that is, meritorious service distinguished by public recognition).

It seems to me that, generally speaking, few things appear to point so patently to the inner corruption of political community life as the skeptical or cynical indifference with which the young generation of today looks upon distinctions bestowed by the state. There may well be valid reason for such skepticism, yet we cannot overlook how disturbingly it reveals the lack of confidence in the fundamental function of the ruler's justice, the act of "distributing." But that is a fresh theme.

At present, however, the main point at issue is the peculiar structure of the act of distributing and, more especially, respect for the person and for his *dignitas*. There are clearly two distinct ways in which we can have respect for a person. One way looks to the person with the aim of effecting just equality; through the other, such equality is completely frustrated. This is the distinction between impartial and partial respect for the person. In the present instance impartial respect is seen to be the specific requirement of distributive justice, partiality its specific ruin. [39]

A moment's thought will show that one of the most easily recognizable characteristics of the contemporary totalitarian constellation of power is expressly to cast suspicion on impartiality and objectivity, while it is part of its program to declare that partiality and "following the party line" constitute the very essence of true public spirit. Such maxims must be considered a threat and temptation to men's political thinking throughout the whole world. They should help us to realize the urgency for restoring in the public's mind the idea of justice as it is formulated in traditional doctrine and contained in the old-fashioned Biblical formula, "respect for the person" (*acceptio personarum*). That expression recurs constantly in both the Old and New Testaments. "Judge that which is just, whether he be of your own country, or a stranger. You shall hear the little as well as the great: neither shall you respect any man's person: because it is the judgment of God." This statement is made in the Book of Deuteronomy (I, 16ff.) in the direction of Moses to the overseers and judges. In the New Testament, in one of Paul's Epistles (Eph. 6, 9), the admonition (likewise directed to the "lords") is found: "Thou knowest that the Lord both of them and you (slaves) is in heaven: and there is no respect of persons with him."

Thomas has devoted a special question to this notion.[40] "It is respect of persons when something is allotted to a person out of proportion to his deserts" (*praeter proportionem dignitatis ipsius*).[41]The typical instance of "respect of persons," and the one which threatens political communal life, is not so much the case in which a man receives (or does not receive) distinction and honor at variance with his true merit. It is rather that public offices and administrative positions are conferred upon men without concern for their qualifications. The *Summa Theologica* sets down in incontrovertible terms what impartial regard for the person and unjust "respect of persons" is. "If you promote a man," Thomas writes,[42]"to a professorship on account of his having sufficient knowledge, you consider the due cause, not the person"—though the candidate must still be examined very thoroughly, and hence, "looked over" very carefully. "But if, in conferring something or someone, you consider in him not the fact that what you give him is proportionate or due to him, but the fact that he is this particular man, Peter or Martin, then there is respect of the person." Or, "if a man promote someone to a prelacy or a professorship because he is rich or because he is a relative of his, it is respect of persons."[43]For the rest, however, Thomas showed realistic restraint in leaving to experience the wholly independent matter of establishing the precise qualifications and merits actually required for a certain post. This refraining from assertion here is part of the matter in hand. Wishing to define a suitable qualification abstractly and "in itself," *simpliciter et secundum se*, is not feasible. Thus a case is quite conceivable in which (in a religious office, for example) a man who is less holy and learned may nevertheless make a greater contribution to the common good—perhaps by virtue of his greater energy and efficiency or because of his "worldly" industry.[44] The same practical wisdom expressed in this remark is repeated in a book on friendship by the Cistercian abbot, Aelred of Rievaulx, in which he says offices must not be bestowed for any reason other than qualifications; for even Christ did not make His favorite disciple, John, the head of His Church.[45]

It is left, then, to *prudentia regnativa*, the prudence of the ruler, and distributive justice to recognize true "worthiness" and to distribute offices and honors in due proportion to real *dignitas*. That means preserving and realizing equality of justice in spite of having respect for persons; for equality will be just as surely violated by respect of persons as it will be by an indiscriminate treatment of everyone which systematically overlooks any and all distinctions.

Justly combining a viewpoint which looks to men's distinctive qualifications and merits with a point of view that considers men's natural equality (for there certainly is a proper worth which is *in the same proportion* in *every* man who bears the countenance of man!) is an almost impossible task. We might say that in this case more than human effort is required. Here we stand in real need of the "favor of the fates" and "the favorable dispensation" of superhuman powers. In a late work of Plato's[46] there is a passage that expresses this point in memorable fashion. Above all else, Plato says, the statesman must constantly keep in mind that justice in virtue of which everyone, though possessed of unequal abilities, receives his due in proportion to his right. But from time to time, so that internal discord within the state may be averted, it is inevitable that equality—"so-called" equality, as Plato terms it—take the place of justice. Occasionally, then, the statesman must make use of the equality of the fates. Yet in so doing he should not neglect to appeal to "God and good fortune," praying that they may let the die fall in the way that is most just. What portion of irony, what of helplessness, and again of trust in the dispensation of the gods, are contained in this Platonic thought—who can tell?

7. *The Limits of Justice*

WE HAVE ALREADY said that it is of the nature of communal life for men constantly to become indebted to each other and then just as constantly to pay one another the debt. We have further said that as a result the balance is in a constant state of shift and needs constantly to be restored to equilibrium. The act of justice is precisely to effect this process of compensations, restitutions, and satisfactions for debts.

It now remains for us to state that the world cannot be kept in order through justice alone. The condition of the historical world is such that the balance cannot always be fully restored through restitution and the paying of debts and dues. The fact that some debts are not or cannot be paid is essential to the world's actual condition. Now there are two aspects to this situation.

Firstly: There are some obligations which, by their very nature, cannot be acquitted in full, much as the one who is thus indebted may be willing to do so. And as justice means to give a person what is due to him, *debitum reddere*, this signifies that there exist relations of indebtedness beyond the scope of the realization of justice. On the other hand, the very relationships which are characterized by this disparity are also the ones fundamental for human existence. And it is naturally the just man, that is, the man who has a firm and constant will to give each man what is his, who will experience that incontrovertible disparity with special acuteness.

It becomes immediately clear that what is meant here is first and foremost man's relation to God. "Whatever man renders to God is due, yet it cannot be equal, as though man rendered to God as much as he owes Him!"[1] This statement is not to be understood as if man were a mere nonentity before God. In a certain sense, Thomas says, something does belong to him, something is "due" to him, which God does give to man. Something belongs to man "by reason of his nature and condition."[2] It is also true that man's nature is created, that is to say, it has not come into existence by reason of anything other than God Himself. "Now the work of divine justice always presupposes the work of mercy; and is founded thereon."[3] This must not be taken to be merely an edifying thought. It is a very precise description of man's condition in the face of God. *Before* any subsequent claim is made by men, indeed even before the mere possibility of such a human claim arises, comes the fact that man has been made a gift by God (of his being) such that his nature cannot ever "make it good," discharge it, "deserve" it, or return it again. Man can never say to God: We are even.

This is the way in which *"religion,"* as a human attitude, is connected with justice. Thomas quite naturally speaks of *religio* within the context of his theory of the virtue of justice. The significance of this connection—and incidentally St. Thomas has been taken to task for making it (the charge being that he "subordinates" religion to one of the acquired virtues) —the significance of this connection is that the inner structure of religious acts first becomes intelligible when man, by reason of his relations with God, has recognized in the disparity between himself and God something which simply cannot be obliterated, a disparity consisting in the fact that a *debitum* exists which his nature cannot repay by any human effort, no matter how heroic it may be, a disparity which simply cannot be overcome. Perhaps it might be possible for contemporary man to gain a view of the reality and significance of *sacrifice* in the cult as a fundamental religious act if he approached it by this rarely traveled path—via the concept of justice, of restitution of something due. From this perspective, it is more easily understood why the offering of sacrifice should be a requirement of justice linked to man's condition as *creatura*. Thomas has actually formulated this point: *Oblatio sacrificii pertinet ad ius naturale*[4]—The obligation of sacrifice is an obligation of natural law. I claim that this doctrine is more easily understood if we set out with the idea of a *debitum* that cannot be repaid, that is, with the notion of an actually existing obligation that nevertheless and by its very nature cannot be wiped out. Here perhaps is the key to the extravagance inherent in religious acts. Helplessness and impotency prompt this extravagance; because it is impossible to do what "properly" ought to be done, an effort beyond the bounds of reason, as it were, tries to compensate for the insufficiency. This explains the excesses of sacrificial offerings such as self-annihilation, killing, burning. Socrates, in the *Gorgias*, says with a most unclassical and indeed an almost unaccountable recklessness (which it would be wrong to interpret simply as an ironical paradox) that a person who has committed injustice must scourge himself, allow himself to be imprisoned, go into exile, accept execution, and yet with all that be the first one to accuse himself, "so that he might be freed from the greatest of evils, from injustice."[5] Here, the old Athenian, who pursued justice with such relentless ardor, speaks from the very same assumption which prompts the doctors of Western Christendom to speak of an *excessus poenitentiae*, an excess proper to the true spirit of penance. In the *Summa Theologica* Thomas formulates the following objection (and it is his answer to this objection which is important to us at this point): The spirit of penance and the spirit of justice are utterly different in that justice clings to the reasonable mean, whereas penance actually consists in an *excessus*. This is his answer to that problem. In certain fundamental relations, for example in man's relation to

God, the equality that properly belongs to the concept of justice, that is, equality between debt and payment, cannot be achieved. Therefore, the one who is in debt strives to pay back whatever is in his power to remit. "Yet this will not be sufficient simply (*simpliciter*). But only according to the acceptance of the higher one, and this is what is meant by ascribing excess to penance," *hoc significatur per excessum, qui attribuitur poenitentiae.*[6] Such *excessus*, then, seems to be a quality of every properly religious act, of sacrifice, adoration, and devotion. It is an attempt to respond to the fact of a relation of indebtedness, an attempt that is the most "adequate" possible under the circumstances, but one that must always remain "inadequate" because it cannot ever achieve a complete *restitutio*. At this point it becomes possible to see why "justice" in the realm of religion can even be perversity, as man boasts of the restitution he makes: "I fast twice in a week. I give tithes of all that I possess" (Luke 18, 12). The true attitude is, rather: "So you also, when you shall have done all these things that are commanded you, say: we are unprofitable servants" (Luke 17, 10).

Thomas speaks of *pietas* as well as of religion. This is a term which cannot be rendered with complete accuracy by our derivation "piety"; and in the discussion which follows it must be remembered that the same applies wherever, for want of a more precise rendering, we have to use the anglicized term. Piety, too, depends on something being due a person which of its very nature cannot be fully repaid. Piety, likewise, is a tendency of the soul which can be fully realized only if man sees himself as the partner in an obligation which can never be truly and fully acquitted, no matter how great the counter-service rendered. "Piety" applies to the parent-child relationship. "It is not possible to make to one's parents an equal return of what one owes to them; and thus piety is annexed to justice."[7] This link indicates that only the just man, in his persistent effort to effect a balance between debts and payments, truly experiences the impossibility of full restitution and "takes it to heart." Piety presupposes the virtue of justice.

Should we set ourselves the task of re-establishing piety as an integral part of the ideal image of man (for it must be frankly admitted that piety is no longer considered a quality necessary to man's "righteousness," nor its lack as indicative of man's inner disorder), the first step would have to be to restore this assumption: that the relation of children to parents might be experienced by the children as an obligation beyond the scope of full restitution. In a word, familial order would have to be restored—in actual fact and in people's estimation. Of course, "familial order" embraces more than the relation between parents and children; but unless it is restored, we cannot expect that the inner experience of an unrepayable obligation should bear as its fruit the feeling of piety.

In speaking of piety, Thomas does not confine himself to the relation between parent and child; he includes man's relation to his country as well. "Man is debtor chiefly to his parents and his country, after God. Wherefore, just as it belongs to religion to give worship to God, so does it belong to piety to give worship to one's parents and one's country."[8] Here we meet with a considerable difficulty. No matter how wide the scope within which we comprise our obligations to our people —counting as goods the language with its inexhaustible treasure of wisdom; the protection afforded by law and order; the participation in whatever can be thought of as the "common good" of a people—yet it remains supremely difficult to accept the thought that it belongs to the image of full and true humanity "to show reverence to one's country," *cultum exhibere patriae*. And as we realize, on further thought, that this difficulty cannot be overcome simply by resolution, that what is implied here goes infinitely beyond the irreverence or the ill-will or the illoyalty of the individual, we begin to measure the extent of the deterioration in the ideal image of man and man's communal life in Western civilization.

This comes into even clearer focus in the third concept Thomas mentions alongside *religio* and *pietas*. It is a concept equally concerned with man's reaction to a condition wherein a debt cannot be canceled. It is the concept of "respect," of *observantia*. The fact that this term has dropped out of current usage, that we have no precise, contemporary equivalent for it, indicates sufficiently that the concept itself has become foreign to us. What, then, does *observantia* mean?

Observantia indicates the respect we feel inwardly and express outwardly toward those persons who are distinguished by their office or by some dignity.[9] We have only to lend an ear to the ironic overtones currently connected with the words "dignity" and "office" to realize at once how remote from us is the reality which Western moral theory has formulated in the concept *observantia* and made an integral part of the ideal image of the ordered man and the ordered community. That theory states that no man can give a recompense equivalent to *virtus*[10]—*virtus* meaning, in this instance, the ability or power (both moral and intellectual) of rightly administering an office. Consequently, a situation arises in which the individual cannot adequately satisfy an obligation. The individual, in his private existence, profits from the proper administration of public offices—by the judge, the teacher, and the like.[11] These men and women create a well-ordered communal life. For this, the individual finds himself indebted to the holders of such offices, in a fashion which cannot be acquitted fully by "payment." It is this situation which is acknowledged by the "respect" shown a person holding an office of public responsibility. The objection that irresponsible and inefficient men may hold offices is of little weight. Thomas's answer is that the office and, in a more general sense, the community as a whole are honored in the person who holds the office.[12]

The root of the matter is here evidently a conception of

man which takes the interdependence of individuals for granted and sees in it nothing shameful or detrimental to the dignity of the person.[13] In any event, within the reality of the world, an ordered community life without leadership and, therefore, without "dependence," is unthinkable. And that holds true of the family as well as of the state—and for the state that is democratically constituted as well as for a dictatorship. Generally speaking, a certain formal structure remains in force at all times and in all places; and if it is not realized in the right way, then it is realized in the wrong way. So that the question can arise whether the void created by the disappearance of the notion of *observantia* (a process certainly not due, however, to mere whim and willfulness) may not have permitted the establishment of another form of relation between superior and subordinate: the shameful expression of mutual contempt which our current jargon renders in the terms "bossing" and "bossed."

This, then, is one aspect of the fact that the world is not to be kept in order through justice alone. There are obligations and debts which of their very nature cannot be adequately fulfilled and discharged. Only the just man takes pains to give each man his due, and only the just man, accordingly, fully experiences that disparity and undertakes to overcome it by some kind of "excess." He fulfills the *debitum* in the clear knowledge that he will never quite succeed in acquitting himself in full measure. For that reason the element of rationality so proper to justice is linked so closely with the exaggeration and, as it were, inadequacy which characterize *religio, pietas,* and *observantia*. All three of these concepts are, therefore, an abomination for rational thought.

Now we can map out a second way of interpreting the proposition of the "limits" of justice. The proposition, in fact, would come to mean that in order to keep the world going, we must be prepared to give what is not in the strictest sense obligatory (whereas, let us remember, the first interpretation of the same proposition was that there are obligations in the strictest sense of the term which man is nonetheless incapable of fulfilling).

The just man, who has a more keenly felt experience of these first inadequacies the more fully he realizes that his very being is a gift, and that he is heavily indebted before God and man, is also the man willing to give where there is no strict obligation He will be willing to give another man something no one can compel him to give. Evidently, there are some actions which one cannot be compelled to perform and which are nonetheless obligatory in the strict sense of the word—telling the truth, for instance. Expressing one's thanks to another is giving him his just due, even though this obviously cannot be enforced. But "being grateful" and "returning thanks" are not of the same order as "paying" and "making restitution." That is why Thomas says, quoting from Seneca, that a person who wants to repay a gift too quickly with a gift in return is an unwilling debtor and an ungrateful person.[14]

So once again, the man who strives for justice, and he above all, realizes (Thomas says) that fulfilling an obligation and doing what he is really obliged to do are not all that is necessary. Something more is required, something over and above, such as liberality, *affabilitas*, kindness, if man's communal life is to remain human. Here nothing more (and certainly nothing *less*) is meant than friendliness in our everyday associations. This "virtue"—and Thomas relates it, too, to justice—is, of course, strictly neither due to another person nor can it be rightfully claimed and demanded. Still it is impossible for men to live together joyfully (*delectabiliter*) without it. "Now as man could not live in society without truth, so likewise not without joy." [15]

I can well imagine how the average young man of our day will respond to these ideas. That he may not enter into them with any great enthusiasm is only to be expected. For the harsher and more "realistic" manner of present-day existence is much more congenial to him. And it is true that we can only with difficulty divest ourselves from the influence of the prevailing atmosphere. Still, it is not the traditional doctrine of justice but precisely our present-day atmosphere which is "unrealistic." That is also the reason why it is so difficult to overcome. But perhaps I may venture the suggestion that one should try, without bias or rash preconceptions, simply to listen to the exposition of the ideal image of justice and follow it through to its final consequence. It is not inconceivable that in the process of listening, it might suddenly become clear that the harsher, more "realistic" approach is nothing but a sign of poverty, of the steadily advancing erosion and aridity of interhuman relationships. It might well become plausible that the manifold and varied forms of partnership of which man is capable (in so far as he is "just") constitute in fact the riches of man and of the human community.

Communal life will necessarily become inhuman if man's dues to man are determined by pure calculation.[16] That the just man give to another what is *not* due to him is particularly important since injustice is the prevailing condition in our world. Because men must do without things that are due to them (since others are withholding them unjustly); since human need and want persist even though no specific person fails to fulfill his obligation, and even though no binding obligation can be construed for anyone; for these very reasons it is not "just and right" for the just man to restrict himself to rendering only what is strictly due. For it is true, as Thomas says, that "mercy without justice is the mother of dissolution"; but, also, that "justice without mercy is cruelty." [17]

Now it becomes possible to state the inner limits of justice: "To be willing to watch over peace and harmony among men through the commandments of justice is not enough when charity has not taken firm root among them."

A Schematic Representation of the Basic Forms of Justice (cf. pp. 73-75)

THE SOCIAL WHOLE

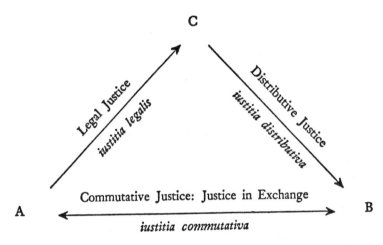

THE INDIVIDUAL PERSON   THE INDIVIDUAL PERSON

FORTITUDE

"*The praise of fortitude is dependent upon justice.*"
ST. THOMAS AQUINAS

1. Readiness to Fall in Battle

FORTITUDE presupposes vulnerability; without vulnerability there is no possibility of fortitude. An angel cannot be brave, because he is not vulnerable. To be brave actually means to be able to suffer injury. Because man is by nature vulnerable, he can be brave.

By injury we understand every assault upon our natural inviolability, every violation of our inner peace; everything that happens to us or is done with us against our will; thus everything in any way negative, everything painful and harmful, everything frightening and oppressive.

The ultimate injury, the deepest injury, is death. And even those injuries which are not fatal are prefigurations of death; this extreme violation, this final negation, is reflected and effective in every lesser injury.

Thus, all fortitude has reference to death. All fortitude stands in the presence of death. Fortitude is basically readiness to die or, more accurately, readiness to fall, to die, in battle.

Every injury to the natural being is fatal in its intention. Thus every courageous action has as its deepest root the readiness to die, even though, viewed from without, it may appear entirely free from any thought of death. Fortitude that does not reach down into the depths of the willingness to die is spoiled at its root and devoid of effective power.

Readiness proves itself in taking a risk, and the culminating point of fortitude is the witness of blood. The essential and the highest achievement of fortitude is martyrdom, and readiness for martyrdom is the essential root of all Christian fortitude. Without this readiness there is no Christian fortitude.

An age that has obliterated from its world view the notion and the actual possibility of martyrdom must necessarily debase fortitude to the level of a swaggering gesture. One must not overlook, however, that this obliteration can be effected in various ways. Next to the timid opinion of the philistine that truth and goodness "prevail of themselves," without demanding any personal commitment, there is the equally pernicious easy enthusiasm which never wearies of proclaiming its "joyful readiness for martyrdom." In both cases, the witness of blood is equally bereft of reality.

The Church thinks otherwise on this matter. On the one hand she declares: Readiness to shed one's blood for Christ is imposed by the strictly binding law of God. "Man must be ready to let himself be killed rather than to deny Christ or to sin grievously." Readiness to die is therefore one of the foundations of Christian life. But as regards a garrulous enthusiasm for martyrdom, let us see what the Church of the martyrs thought about it. In the "Martyrdom of St. Polycarp," one of the oldest accounts from the period of persecution (about A.D. 150), sent by the "Church of God in Smyrna" to "all congregations of the holy and Catholic Church," a brief paragraph is explicit:

"But one, a Phrygian called Quintus, became afraid when he saw the wild animals. It was this very man who had presented himself voluntarily to the court and persuaded others to do the same. By repeated urging the Proconsul brought him to sacrifice and to forswear Christ. Therefore, brethren, we have no praise for those who offer themselves voluntarily; this is not the counsel of the Gospel." [2]

The Church Father St. Cyprian, who was beheaded in 258, declared to the Consul Paternus: "Our teaching forbids anyone to report himself." [3] It appears that the Fathers of the ancient Church, from St. Cyprian to St. Gregory of Nazianzus and St. Ambrose, actually assumed that God would most readily withdraw the strength of endurance from those who, arrogantly trusting their own resolve, thrust themselves into martyrdom. Finally, St. Thomas Aquinas, in whose *Summa* an article deals with the so-called "joys of fortitude," says that the pain of martyrdom obscures even the spiritual joy in an act pleasing to God, "unless the overflowing grace of God lift the soul with exceeding strength to things divine." [4]

In the face of the unromantic, harsh reality expressed in these grave statements, all bombastic enthusiasm and oversimplification vanish into thin air. In this, then, does the actual significance of the unyielding fact that the Church counts readiness to shed one's blood among the foundations of Christian life become clearly manifest.

The suffering of injury is only a partial and foreground aspect of fortitude. The brave man suffers injury not for its own sake, but rather as a means to preserve or to acquire a deeper, more essential intactness.

Christian consciousness has never lost the certainty that an injury suffered in fighting for the good confers an intactness which is more closely and intimately related to the core of man's life than all purely natural serenity, though critics and opponents of Christianity have not always succeeded in recognizing and correctly estimating either this certainty or its rank among Christian vital forces.

To the early Church, martyrdom appeared as a victory, even though a fatal one. "He conquers for the Faith by his death; living without the Faith he would be conquered," [5] says St. Maximus of Turin, a bishop of the fifth century, concerning the witness of blood. And in Tertullian we read: "We are victorious when we are stricken down; we escape when we are led before the judge." [6]

The fact that these victories are fatal or at least harmful belongs to the incomprehensible and immutable conditions under which the Christian—and perhaps not only he—exists in the world. Thomas Aquinas seems to consider it to be almost the nature of fortitude that it fights against the *superior* power of evil, which the brave man can defeat only by his death or injury. We shall take up this thought again later.

First and foremost: the brave man does not suffer injury for its own sake. For the Christian no less than for the "natural" man, "suffering for its own sake" is nonsense. The Christian does not despise the things that are destroyed by injury. The martyr does not simply consider life of little worth, though he does value it cheaper than that for which he sacrifices it. The Christian loves his life, says Thomas, not only with the natural, life-asserting forces of the body, but with the moral forces of the spiritual soul as well. Nor is this said by way of apology. Man loves his natural life not because he is "a mere man"; he loves it because and to the extent that he is a *good* man.[7] The same applies not only to life itself, but to everything included in the range of natural intactness: joy, health, success, happiness. All these things are genuine goods, which the Christian does not toss aside and esteem but lightly—unless, indeed, to preserve higher goods, the loss of which would injure more deeply the inmost core of human existence.

The validity of all this is not impaired by the fact that obviously the heroic life of the saints and great Christians is far more than the result of a carefully calculated reckoning of profit and loss.

This "tension" cannot be resolved in harmony; for the temporal intellect and earthly existence it is irreversible and absolute. But it is neither more nor less contradictory than the sentence from the Gospels: Whoever loves his life will lose it (John 12, 25). Nor is it more enigmatic than the astonishing fact that a man as open to reality and to the world as Thomas

Aquinas, who so often is quoted in support of practical optimism, also teaches: The truly penetrating knowledge of created things is associated with an abysmal sadness, an insuperable sadness which cannot be lifted by any natural force of knowledge or will (according to Thomas it is this sadness the Sermon of the Mount refers to when it is said: Blessed are those who mourn, for they shall be comforted).

To try to cross the border into the unknowable is a hopeless endeavor. These questions concerning the meaning and measure of the sacrifice of natural goods lead directly into the impenetrable mystery inherent in the human condition: the existence of a being both corporal and spiritual, created, elevated, fallen, redeemed.

2. Fortitude Must Not Trust Itself

IF THE SPECIFIC CHARACTER of fortitude consists in suffering injuries in the battle for the realization of the good, then the brave man must first know what the good is, and he must be brave for the sake of the good. "It is for the sake of the good that the brave man exposes himself to the danger of death." [1]"In overcoming danger, fortitude seeks not danger itself, but the realization of rational good."[2]"To take death upon oneself is not in itself praiseworthy, but solely because of its subordination to good."[3] It is not the injury that matters primarily, but the realization of the good.

Therefore fortitude, though it puts man to the severest test, is not the first and greatest of the virtues. For neither difficulty nor effort causes virtue, but the good alone.[4]

Fortitude therefore points to something prior. Essentially it is something secondary, subordinate, deriving its measure from something else. It has its place in a scale of meaning and value where it does not rank first. Fortitude is not independent, it does not stand by itself. It receives its proper significance only in relation to something other than itself.

"Fortitude must not trust itself," says Ambrose.[5]

Every child knows that in the list of cardinal virtues fortitude comes third. This enumeration is not accidental: it is a meaningfully graded series.

Prudence and justice precede fortitude. And that means, categorically: without prudence, without justice, there is no fortitude; only he who is just and prudent can also be brave; to be really brave is quite impossible without at the same time being prudent and just also.

Nor is it possible to discuss the nature of fortitude without examining its relation to prudence and justice.

To begin with, only the prudent man can be brave. Fortitude without prudence is not fortitude.

The growing surprise we experience as we examine this proposition more closely marks the measure of our estrangement from the self-evident foundations of the classical teachings of the Church on human life. Only recently have we hesitantly begun to rediscover what is expressed in this proposition, namely, the proper place and the high rank that belong to prudence.

To mention fortitude and prudence in the same breath seems in a measure to contradict modern man's notion of prudence and also of fortitude. This is partially due to the fact that current usage does not designate quite the same thing by "prudence" as classical theology understood by *prudentia* and *discretio*. The term "prudence" has come to mean rather the slyness which permits the cunning and "shrewd" tactician to evade any dangerous risk to his person, and thus escape injury and even the possibility of injury. To us, prudence seems to be that false "discretion" and "cool consideration" conjured up by the coward in order to be able to shirk the test. To "prudence" thus conceived, fortitude seems plainly unwise or stupid.

In truth, fortitude becomes fortitude only through being "informed" by prudence. The double meaning of "inform" is here very apt. "Inform" in the current usage means primarily "instruct"; secondly, as a technical term of scholasticism, taken directly from the Latin *informare*, it means "to give inner form to." Referring to the relation between prudence and fortitude, the two meanings interlock: in the instruction of fortitude by prudence the former receives from the latter its inner form, that is, its specific character as a virtue.

The virtue of fortitude has nothing to do with a purely vital, blind, exuberant, daredevil spirit. (On the other hand it presupposes a healthy vitality, perhaps more than any other virtue.) The man who recklessly and indiscriminately courts any kind of danger is not for that reason brave; all he proves is that, without preliminary examination or distinction, he considers all manner of things more valuable than the personal intactness which he risks for their sake.[6] The nature of fortitude is not determined by risking one's person arbitrarily, but only by a sacrifice of self in accordance with reason, that is, with the true nature and value of real things. "Not in any way whatsoever, but according to reason."[7] Genuine fortitude presupposes a correct evaluation of things, of the things that one risks as well as of those which one hopes to preserve or gain by the risk.

Pericles, in the lofty words of his speech for the fallen heroes, expressed Christian wisdom also: "For this too is our way: to dare most liberally where we have reflected best. With others, only ignorance begets fortitude; and reflection but begets hesitation." [8]

Prudence gives their inner form to all the other cardinal virtues: justice, fortitude, and temperance. But these three are not equally dependent upon prudence. Fortitude is less directly informed by prudence than justice; justice is the first word of prudence, fortitude the second; prudence informs fortitude, as it were, through justice. Justice is based solely upon the recognition of reality achieved by prudence; fortitude, however, is based upon prudence and justice together.

Thomas Aquinas gives the following explanation for the hierarchy of the cardinal virtues: the actual good of man is his self-realization in accordance with reason, that is, in accordance with the truth of real things. (Let us keep in mind that for the classical theology of the Church, reason always and only means the "passage" to reality. We must avoid the temptation of transferring our justifiably contemptuous lack of confidence in the dictatorial "reason" of the idealist philosophers of the nineteenth century to the *ratio* of scholasticism, always closely related to reality.) The essence of this "good of reason" is conferred in the directive cognition of prudence. In the virtue of justice, this good of reason becomes transformed into actual existence. "It is the function of justice to carry out the order of reason in all human affairs." The other virtues—fortitude and temperance—serve the conservation of this good; it is their function to preserve man from declining from the good. Among these two latter virtues, fortitude takes precedence.[9]

Under the direction of prudence, the good of man becomes compellingly evident. Justice primarily brings about the actual realization of this good. Fortitude therefore, by itself, is not the primary realization of the good. But fortitude protects this realization or clears the road for it.

So we cannot simply say that only the prudent man can be brave. We have further to see that a "fortitude" which is not subservient to justice is just as false and unreal as a "fortitude" which is not informed by prudence.

Without the "just cause" there is no fortitude. "Not the injury, but the cause makes martyrs," says St. Augustine.[10] "Man does not expose his life to mortal danger, except to maintain justice. Therefore the praise of fortitude depends upon justice," says St. Thomas.[11] And in his *Book of Duties*, St. Ambrose says: "Fortitude without justice is a lever of evil."[12]

3. *Endurance and Attack*

TO BE BRAVE is not the same as to have no fear. Indeed, fortitude actually rules out a certain kind of fearlessness, namely the sort of fearlessness that is based upon a false appraisal and evaluation of reality. Such fearlessness is either blind and deaf to real danger, or else it is the result of a perversion of love. For fear and love depend upon each other: a person who does not love, does not fear either, and he who loves falsely, fears falsely. One who has lost the will to live does not fear death. But this indifference to life is far removed from genuine fortitude; it is, indeed, an inversion of the natural order. Fortitude recognizes, acknowledges, and maintains the natural order of things. The brave man is not deluded: he sees that the injury he suffers is an evil. He does not undervalue and falsify reality; he "likes the taste" of reality as it is, real; he does not love death nor does he despise life. Fortitude presupposes in a certain sense that man is afraid of evil; its essence lies not in knowing no fear, but in not allowing oneself to be forced into evil by fear, or to be kept by fear from the realization of good.

Whoever exposes himself to a danger—even for the sake of good—without knowledge of its perils, either from instinctive optimism ("nothing can possibly happen to *me*") or from firm confidence in his own natural strength and fighting fitness, does not on that account possess the virtue of fortitude.[1]

It is possible to be genuinely brave only when all those real or apparent assurances fail, that is, when the natural man is afraid; not, however, when he is afraid out of unreasoning timidity, but when, with a clear view of the real situation facing him, he cannot help being afraid, and, indeed, with good reason. If in this supreme test, in face of which the braggart falls silent and every heroic gesture is paralyzed, a man walks straight up to the cause of his fear and is not deterred from doing that which is good; if, moreover, he does so for the sake of good—which ultimately means for the sake of God, and therefore not from ambition or from fear of being taken for a coward—this man, and he alone, is truly brave.

To maintain this position is not to depreciate in the least the value of natural optimism and natural strength and fighting fitness; neither is their vital significance or their great ethical importance thereby diminished. It is, however, important to understand wherein lies the actual nature of fortitude as a virtue, and to realize that it lies beyond the realm of the merely vital. In the face of martyrdom, all natural optimism becomes senseless, and the hands of the man most fit for battle are, literally, tied. But as martyrdom is the essential and the highest achievement of fortitude, it is only in this supreme test that its true nature stands revealed and the yardstick for its less heroic realizations is provided (for it belongs to the nature of virtue to fix its gaze upon the ultimate). [2]

Fortitude consequently does not mean mere fearlessness. That man alone is brave who cannot be forced, through fear of transitory and lesser evils, to give up the greater and actual good, and thereby bring upon himself that which is ultimately and absolutely dreadful. This fear of the ultimately dreadful belongs, as the "reverse" of the love of God, to the absolutely necessary foundations of fortitude (and of all virtue): "He who feareth the Lord will tremble at *nothing*" (Eccles. 34, 16).

So whoever realizes the good by facing what is dreadful, by facing injury, is truly brave. This "facing" the dreadful has two aspects, which form the foundation for the two basic acts of fortitude: endurance and attack.

Endurance is more of the essence of fortitude than attack. This proposition of St. Thomas[3] may seem strange to us, and many of our contemporaries may glibly dismiss it as the expression of a "typically medieval" "passivist" philosophy and doctrine. Such an interpretation, however, would hit wide of the mark. Thomas in no way means to rate endurance in itself higher than attack, or to propose that in every case it is braver to endure than to attack. What, then, does his proposition mean? It can mean only that the true "position" of fortitude is that extremely perilous situation described above, in which to suffer and endure is objectively the only remaining possibility of resistance, and that it is in this situation that fortitude primarily and ultimately proves its genuine character. It is of course an integral part of St. Thomas's conception of the world, of the Christian conception of the world, that man may be placed in a position to be injured or killed for the realization of the good and that evil, considered in terms of this world, may appear as an overwhelming power. This possibility, we know, has been obliterated from the world view of enlightened liberalism.

To suffer and endure is, furthermore, something passive only in an external sense. Thomas himself raises the objection: If fortitude is a perfection, then how can enduring be its essential act? For enduring is pure passivity, and active doing is more perfect than passive suffering. And he replies: Enduring comprises a strong activity of the soul, namely, a vigorous grasping of and clinging to the good; and only from this stouthearted activity can the strength to support the physical and spiritual suffering of injury and death be nourished.[4] It cannot be denied that a timid Christianity, overwhelmed and frightened by the un-Christian criteria of an ideal of fortitude that is activistically heroic, has smothered this fact in the general consciousness, and misconstrued it in the sense of a vague and resentful passivism.

The same applies, and even to a higher degree, to the current notion of the virtue of patience. For Thomas, patience is a necessary component of fortitude. We are apt to regard this co-ordination of patience with fortitude as incongruous, not only because we easily mistake the nature of fortitude for activism, but first and foremost because in our conception patience (in sharp contrast to the ideas of classical theology) has come to mean an indiscriminate, self-immolating, crabbed, joyless, and spineless submission to whatever evil is met with or, worse, deliberately sought out. Patience, however, is something quite other than the indiscriminate acceptance of any and every evil: "The patient man is not the one who does not flee from evil, but the one who does not allow himself to be made inordinately sorrowful thereby."[5] To be patient means to preserve cheerfulness and serenity of mind in spite of injuries that result from the realization of the good. Patience does not imply the exclusion of energetic, forceful activity, but simply, explicitly and solely the exclusion of sadness and confusion of heart.[6] Patience keeps man from the danger that his spirit may be broken by grief and lose its greatness.[7] Patience, therefore, is not the tear-veiled mirror of a "broken" life (as one might easily assume in the face of what is frequently presented and praised under this name), but the radiant embodiment of ultimate integrity. In the words of Hildegard of Bingen, patience is "the pillar which nothing can soften."[8] And Thomas, following Holy Scripture (Luke 21, 19), summarizes with superb precision: "Through patience man possesses his soul." [9]

The man who is brave is for that very reason patient as well. But the reverse proposition cannot be said to be true: patience by itself does not constitute the whole of fortitude,[10] no more, nay, less than does endurance, to which patience is subordinated. The brave man not only knows how to bear inevitable evil with equanimity; he will also not hesitate to "pounce upon" evil and to bar its way, if this can reasonably be done. This attitude requires readiness to attack, courage, self-confidence, and hope of success; "the trust that is a part of fortitude signifies the hope which a man puts in himself: naturally in subordination to God."[11] These things are so self-evident that we need not waste words upon them.

The fact, however, that Thomas assigns to (just) wrath a positive relation to the virtue of fortitude has become largely unintelligible and unacceptable to present-day Christianity and its non-Christian critics. This lack of comprehension may be explained partly by the exclusion, from Christian ethics, of the component of passion (with its inevitably physical aspect) as something alien and incongruous—an exclusion due to a kind of intellectual stoicism—and partly by the fact that the explosive activity which reveals itself in wrath is naturally repugnant to good behavior regulated by "bourgeois" standards. So Thomas, who is equally free from both these errors, says: The brave man uses wrath for his own act, above all in attack, "for it is peculiar to wrath to pounce upon evil. Thus fortitude and wrath work directly upon each other."[12]

Not only as regards the "passive," but also as regards the pronouncedly "aggressive," the classical doctrine of fortitude exceeds the narrow range of conventional notions.

Yet the fact remains that that which is preponderantly of the essence of fortitude is neither attack nor self-confidence nor wrath, but endurance and patience. Not because (and this cannot be sufficiently stressed) patience and endurance are in themselves better and more perfect than attack and self-confidence, but because, in the world as it is constituted, it is only in the supreme test, which leaves no other possibility of resistance than endurance, that the inmost and deepest strength of man reveals itself. Power is so manifestly of the very structure of the world that endurance, not wrathful attack, is the ultimately decisive test of actual fortitude, which, essentially, is nothing else than to love and to realize that which is good, in the face of injury or death, and undeterred by any spirit of compromise. It is one of the fundamental laws of a world plunged into disorder by original sin that the uttermost strength of the good manifests itself in powerlessness. And the Lord's words, "Behold, I send you as sheep among wolves" (Matt. 10, 16), continue to mark the position of the Christian in the world, even to this day.

This thought and this reality may appear virtually unacceptable to each "new generation." The reluctance to acknowledge them and the inner revolt against the "resignation" of those who have "resigned themselves" are, indeed, hallmarks of genuine youthfulness. In this revolt, at least, there lives the ineradicable human sense of the original and essential order of creation, an intimation that no genuine Christian can lose, even though he has learned to acknowledge the spiritually inevitable disorder caused by original sin, not only as an idea to be conceived but as a reality to be experienced. Implicit in the aforesaid is the fact that there are also non-Christian or pre-Christian modes of "putting up with" which it may be the perpetual mission of youth to overcome, and specifically of Christian youth.

Further: the figure of the "sheep among wolves" refers above all to the hidden depth of Christian existence in the world, although, as an actual possibility, it forms the foundation of all concrete conflicts, determining and coloring them all. It is disclosed in its naked and absolute reality, however, only in cases of the supreme test; then, indeed, the pure and unadulterated realization of this figure is demanded of every Christian. On the surface, above this depth, there lies the broad field of active worldly endeavor and the struggle for the realization of the good against the opposition of stupidity, laziness, blindness, and malevolence. Christ Himself, of whom the Fathers of the Church say that His agony is the source of the strength of the martyrs,[13] and whose earthly life was entirely permeated and formed by His readiness for sacrificial death, to which He went "like a lamb to the slaughter"—Christ drove the money-changers from the temple with a whip; and when the most patient of men stood before the high priest and was struck in the face by a servant, He did *not* turn the other cheek, but answered: "If there was harm in what I said, tell us what was harmful in it, but if not, why dost thou strike me?" (John 18, 23).

Thomas Aquinas, in his commentary on St. John's Gospel, has pointed to the apparent contradiction between this scene (as well as the one from the Acts of the Apostles, referred to below) and the injunction of the Sermon on the Mount: "I say unto you, resist not evil; if one strike you on the right cheek, offer him the other" (Matt. 5, 39). A passivistic exegesis is quite unable to solve this "contradiction." Thomas explains (in agreement with Augustine): "Holy Scripture must be understood in the light of what Christ and the saints have actually practiced. Christ did not offer His other cheek, nor Paul either. Thus to interpret the injunction of the Sermon on the Mount *literally* is to misunderstand it. This injunction signifies rather the readiness of the soul to bear, *if it be necessary*, such things and worse, without bitterness against the attacker. This readiness our Lord showed, when He gave up His body to be crucified. That response of the Lord was useful, therefore, for our instruction."[14]

Similarly, the Apostle Paul, although his whole life was oriented toward martyrdom, did not suffer it in silence when, at the command of the high priest, he was "struck on the mouth" by the bystanders for his bold speech before the Sanhedrin; rather, he answered the high priest: "It is God that will smite thee for the whitened wall that thou art; thou art sitting there to judge me according to the law, and wilt thou break the law by ordering them to smite me?" (Acts 23, 3).

The readiness to meet the supreme test by dying in patient endurance so that the good may be realized does not exclude the willingness to fight and to attack. Indeed, it is from this readiness that the springs of action in the Christian receive that detachment and freedom which, in the last analysis, are denied to every sort of tense and strained activism.

4. Vital, Moral, Mystic Fortitude

THE VIRTUE OF FORTITUDE keeps man from so loving his life that he loses it.

This principle—that he who loves his life loses it—is valid for every order of human reality: in the "pre-moral" order of mental health, in the actually "moral" order of natural ethics, in the "supermoral" order of supernatural life. In all three orders, therefore, a special significance attaches to fortitude. Only in the second order is it a "human virtue" in the strict sense; in the first it ranks below, and in the third, above it.

All three orders can be clearly separated only in the mind; in the reality of human existence they interlock. No one can say in a specific case where the sphere of moral guilt ends and the sphere of mental and psychical illness begins; and in the Christian era there is no such thing as "purely natural" virtue without actual reference to the order of grace. Thus fortitude, too, ranges through all these orders in what may be called a unified human attitude of mind and being.

To the modern science of psychology, we owe the insight that the lack of courage to accept injury and the incapability of self-sacrifice belong to the deepest sources of psychic illness. All neuroses seem to have as a common symptom an egocentric anxiety, a tense and self-centered concern for security, the inability to "let go"; in short, that kind of love for one's own life that leads straight to the loss of life. It is a very significant and by no means accidental fact that modern psychology frequently quotes the Scriptural words: "He who loves his life will lose it." Above and beyond their immediate religious significance they denote accurately the psychiatric-characterological diagnosis: that "the ego will become involved in ever greater danger the more carefully one tries to protect it." [1]

This pre-moral fortitude, as a source of psychic health closely connected with the sphere of vitality, is, in a manner beyond conscious control, linked to, and permeated by, properly moral fortitude; the moral force which, by virtue of *anima forma corporis*, works its formative effect in the sphere of the natural. On the other hand, and in a no less complicated interplay, the pre-moral fortitude seems to be the prerequisite and foundation of the essential spiritual fortitude of the man and the Christian, which grows from the soil of a fortitude rooted in the vital forces.

Christian fortitude, in the spiritual and intellectual sense, develops in proportion to the degrees of perfection proper to the interior life.

Although the supernatural ranks in essence incomparably higher than the order of nature, the former is, to begin with, less perfectly "in the possession" of man. The natural vital powers of body and mind are man's immediate and, so to speak, wholly subservient property; the supernatural life of faith, hope, and charity is only indirectly his own. Only by the unfolding of the gifts of the Holy Ghost, which are bestowed on the Christian together with the theological virtue of charity, can supernatural life become our "full possession" to such an extent that, as second nature, it urges us as though "naturally" on to sanctity. [2]

Accordingly, the degrees of perfection of Christian fortitude correspond to the degrees of unfolding of the gift of fortitude—the fortitude we owe to grace, and which belongs to the seven gifts of the Holy Ghost.

St. Thomas Aquinas distinguishes three degrees of perfection in fortitude (as in all cardinal virtues). The lowest—which on the next higher degree is not "left behind" but absorbed—is the "political" fortitude of everyday, normal community life. Almost everything that has so far been said about fortitude (excepting the references to martyrdom) applies to this—in the Christian sense—initial degree. On the road to inner progress from the first to the second and "purgatorial" purifying degree of fortitude, the man intent on a higher realization of the divine image in himself crosses the threshold of the properly mystical life. Mystical life, however, is nothing but the more perfect unfolding of the supernatural love of God and of the gifts of the Holy Ghost. The third degree of fortitude—the fortitude of the purified spirit already transformed in its essence—is attained only on the greatest heights of earthly sanctity, which are already a beginning of eternal life.[3]

Of "purgatorial fortitude," which for the average Christian represents the highest attainable degree of fortitude, Thomas says that it gives the soul the power to remain undaunted by its entrance into the higher world.[4] At first glance this seems to be a very strange proposition. But it becomes more intelligible when one considers the unanimous experience of all great mystics: at the beginning and before the final perfection of the mystic life, the soul is exposed as to a "dark night" of the senses and the spirit, in which it must think itself abandoned and lost like a man drowning on the open sea. St. John of the Cross, the mystic doctor, says that in the "dark fire" of this night—which is a true purgatory whose torment ineffably exceeds any self-imposed penance that an ascetic could imagine

—God cleanses with inexorably healing hand the senses and the spirit from the dross of sin.

The Christian who dares to take the leap into this darkness and relinquishes the hold of his anxiously grasping hand, totally abandoning himself to God's absolute control, thus realizes in a very strict sense the nature of fortitude; for the sake of love's perfection he walks straight up to dreadfulness; he is not afraid to lose his life for Life's sake; he is ready to be slain by the sight of the Lord ("No man beholdeth me and liveth" —Ex. 33, 20).

At this point the true significance of the expression "heroic virtue" first becomes evident: the basis of this stage of the inner life, whose nature is the unfolding of the gifts of the Holy Ghost,[5] is in fact fortitude, the virtue which is in a very special sense, primarily and by name, an "heroic" virtue, that is, the fortitude exalted by grace, the fortitude of the mystic life. The great teacher of Christian mysticism, Teresa of Ávila, says that fortitude ranks first and foremost among the prerequisites of perfection. In her autobiography we find the decisively formulated statement: "I assert that an imperfect human being needs more fortitude to pursue the way of perfection than suddenly to become a martyr." [6]

On this higher degree of fortitude, which the martyr attains, as it were, in one powerful, audacious leap, the natural forces of endurance fail. They are replaced by the Holy Spirit of fortitude, which works "in us without us" that we may overcome the darkness and reach the steep shore of light. When, in the experience of extreme anguish, the strengthening and comforting illumination of natural certainties—the metaphysical ones not excepted—wanes and changes into the half-light of uncertainty, He gives man that unshakable though veiled supernatural certainty of the final happy victory, without which, in the supernatural order, battle and injury are objectively unbearable. In the gift of fortitude the Holy Spirit pours into the soul a confidence that overcomes all fear: namely, that He will lead man to eternal life, which is the goal and purpose of all good actions, and the final deliverance from every kind of danger. [7]

This superhuman mode of fortitude is in the absolute sense a "gift." The doctors of the Church have always applied to its victories the following words of Scripture: "For they got not possession of the land by their own sword: neither did their own arm save them. But thy right hand and thy arm, and the light of thy countenance: because thou wast pleased with them" (Psalm 43).

St. Augustine and St. Thomas associate with the spiritual gift of fortitude the beatitude "Blessed are they who hunger and thirst for justice, for they shall be filled."

The supernatural gift of fortitude by no means frees the Christian from hunger and thirst for justice; it does not release him from the painful necessity of taking upon himself, in the battle for the realization of good, injury—and even, in extreme cases, death. But the doctrinal truth of ultimate "satiation," which is only "theoretically" known and possessed at the initial stages of fortitude and of the interior life in general, rises at this higher stage to an evidence so direct and compelling as to resemble the experience of sight, hearing, and touch in the natural order: so that on the deepest ground of hunger and thirst, which incidentally lose nothing of their consuming reality, the overwhelming certainty of "being filled" flashes forth in such triumphant reality that this certainty is itself "blessedness."

These three basic forms of human fortitude—the pre-moral, the properly ethical, and the mystical—all realize the same essential image: man accepts insecurity; he surrenders confidently to the governance of higher powers; he "risks" his immediate well-being; he abandons the tense, egocentric hold of a timorous anxiety. The uniformity of this attitude of mind and being, which underlies all three modes of fortitude, exists in spite of the differences that separate the sphere of mental health from those of the morally good and of the mystic life. These differences are real, and they should not be blurred. But the tendency has been too often to isolate each sphere from the others. Their inner, essential, and reciprocal connections have not been sufficiently noticed. For they it is which, in the concrete reality of human existence, relate the vital and the psychical spheres to the moral and mystic ones—in a manner, however, whose complicated interactions we in all probability will never wholly grasp.

Whoever, in the vital and psychical sphere, egocentrically strains toward complete security for himself, and is incapable of daring a venturesome undertaking, will presumably also fail when to realize the good demands the suffering of injury or, worse, of death. But here we touch a sphere in which that which is essential is never wont to appear.

With this weighty reservation in mind, it may now be said that an education aiming at the development of physical courage (which ought not to be simply equated with "physical training") belongs in a specific sense to the essential foundation of moral fortitude. On the other hand, the cure of a mental illness which has overanxiety as its root, will rarely be successful without the simultaneous moral "conversion" of the whole man. This in turn, for the eye firmly directed on concrete existence, cannot develop in an area cut off from grace, the sacraments, the mystical life.

This living connection of moral fortitude in the stricter sense with supermoral fortitude of the mystic order is of the very greatest importance. Notably departing from the classical theology of the Church, the moral teachings of the last century have separated mystical life as in essence "extraordinary" from the "ordinary" ethical sphere, and have consequently obstructed our view of the continuity in the unfolding of the supernatural life.

It is clear that political fortitude, which consists mainly in combating outward resistance in order to help justice to realization, is of a different order than "mystic" fortitude, by virtue of which the soul, for the sake of union with God, ventures into the painful darkness of "passive purification." But quite apart from the consideration that the same basic human attitude of abandonment of self is realized in both kinds of fortitude, one must not overlook the fact that the more strictly moral fortitude of the Christian reaches essentially beyond itself, into the mystic order, which, as has been said repeatedly, is nothing other than the more perfect unfolding of the supernatural life that every Christian receives in baptism. Mystic fortitude, on the other hand, reaches so effectively into the moral (and the vital-psychical) sphere, that one may say that the inmost strength of "political" fortitude derives from the hidden abandonment of man to God, from his unconditional acceptance of insecurity, which is the risk one must take in the mystical life.

Wherever a "new generation" takes up the attack against the resisting forces of evil or against a tense obsession with a security which clings to the delusion that the disharmony of the world is fundamentally curable by cautious and correct "tactics," it is above all necessary to maintain a lively and vigilant awareness that such fighting can only reach beyond sound and fury if it draws its strongest forces from the fortitude of the mystical life, which dares to submit unconditionally to the governance of God. Without a consciously preserved connection with these reserves of strength, all struggle for the good must lose its genuineness and the inner conviction of victory, and in the end can lead only to the noisy sterility of spiritual pride.

The supernatural fortitude bestowed by grace, which is a gift of the Holy Spirit, pervades and crowns all other "natural" modes of Christian fortitude. For to be brave means not only to suffer injury and death in the struggle for the realization of the good, but also to hope for victory. Without this hope, fortitude is impossible. And the higher this victory, the more certain the hope for it, the more man risks to gain it. The supernatural gift of fortitude, the gift of the Holy Spirit, however, is nourished by the surest hope of the final and highest victory, in which all other victories, by their hidden reference to it, are perfected—the hope of life eternal.

No doubt to die without hope is harder and more fearful than dying in the hope of eternal life. But who would be willing to accept such nonsense as this: that it is braver to enter death without hope? Yet whoever takes not the *end* but the *effort* as the good can hardly avoid this nihilistic conclusion. As St. Augustine says, it is not injury that makes the martyr, but the fact that his action is in accordance with truth. What matters is not the ease or the difficulty, but "the truth of things." What matters is the reality of eternal life. And the "rectitude" of hope lies in the fact that it corresponds to this reality.

On the other hand, it is hope that, in the case of martyrdom, is put to its most revealing and unsparing test. It is one thing to say and suppose that one lives in hope of life eternal, and it is another thing really to hope. What hope actually is, no one can know more profoundly than he who must prove himself in the supreme test of ultimate fortitude. And to no other will it be more convincingly revealed that hope for eternal life is properly a gift, and that without this gift there can be no such thing as truly Christian fortitude.

TEMPERANCE

1. Temperance and Moderation

WHAT HAVE THE WORDS "temperance" and "moderation" come to mean in today's parlance?

The meaning of "temperance" has dwindled miserably to the crude significance of "temperateness in eating and drinking." We may add that this term is applied chiefly, if not exclusively, to the designation of mere quantity, just as "intemperance" seems to indicate only excess. Needless to say, "temperance" limited to this meaning cannot even remotely hint at the true nature of *temperantia*, to say nothing of expressing its full content. *Temperantia* has a wider significance and a higher rank: it is a cardinal virtue, one of the four hinges on which swings the gate of life.

Nor does "moderation" correspond to the meaning and rank of *temperantia*. Moderation mainly relates to admonishing the wrathful to moderate their anger. Though the moderation of anger belongs to the realm of *temperantia*, it is only a part of it. If we leave the tepid atmosphere of a moral theology mistrustful of all passion to enter the more realistic and bracing climate of the *Summa Theologica*, we find, surprisingly, that the *passio* of anger is defended rather than condemned. Further: the current concept of moderation is dangerously close to fear of any exuberance. We all know that the term "prudent moderation" tends to crop up when the love of truth or some other generous impulse threatens to take an extreme risk. This emasculated concept of moderation has no place in a doctrine which asserts that the love of God—fountainhead of all virtues

—knows neither mean nor measure. "Moderation," also, is too negative in its implication and signifies too exclusively restriction, curtailment, curbing, bridling, repression—all again in contradiction to the classic prototype of the fourth cardinal virtue.

A study of the linguistic meaning of the Greek term, *sophrosyne,* and of the Latin *temperantia* reveals a much wider range of significance. The original meaning of the Greek word embraces "directing reason" in the widest sense. And the Latin stays close to this far-ranging significance. In St. Paul's First Epistle to the Corinthians (12, 24f.) we read: *Deus temperavit corpus.* "Thus God has established a harmony in the body, giving special honor to that which needed it most. There was to be no want of unity in the body; all the different parts of it were to make each other's welfare their common care." The primary and essential meaning of *temperare,* therefore, is this: to dispose various parts into one unified and ordered whole.

2. Selfless Self-Preservation

AQUINAS SAYS that the second meaning of temperance is "serenity of the spirit" (*quies animi*).[1] It is obvious that this proposition does not imply a purely subjective state of mental calm or the tranquil satisfaction which is the by-product of an unassuming, leisurely life in a narrow circle. Nor does it mean a mere absence of irritation, or dispassionate equanimity. All this need not go deeper than the surface of the intellectual and spiritual life. What is meant is the serenity that fills the inmost recesses of the human being, and is the seal and fruit of order. The purpose and goal of *temperantia* is man's inner order, from which alone this "serenity of spirit" can flow forth. "Temperance" signifies the realizing of this order within oneself.

Temperantia is distinguished from the other cardinal virtues by the fact that it refers exclusively to the active man himself. Prudence looks to all existent reality; justice to the fellow man; the man of fortitude relinquishes, in self-forgetfulness, his own possessions and his life. Temperance, on the other hand, aims at each man himself.[2] Temperance implies that man should look to himself and his condition, that his vision and his will should be focused on himself. That notion that the primordial images of all things reside in God has been applied by Aquinas to the cardinal virtues also: the primordial divine mode of *temperantia,* he states, is the "turning of the Divine Spirit to Itself." [3]

For man there are two modes of this turning toward the self: a selfless and a selfish one. Only the former makes for self-preservation; the latter is destructive. In modern psychology we find this thought: genuine self-preservation is the turning of man toward himself, with the essential stipulation, however, that in this movement he does not become fixed upon himself. ("Whoever fixes his eyes upon himself gives no light.") Temperance is selfless self-preservation. Intemperance is self-destruction through the selfish degradation of the powers which aim at self-preservation.

It is a commonplace though nonetheless mysterious truth that man's inner order—unlike that of the crystal, the flower, or the animal—is not a simply given and self-evident reality, but rather that the same forces from which human existence derives its being can upset that inner order to the point of destroying the spiritual and moral person. That this cleavage in human nature (provided we do not try to persuade ourselves that it does not exist) finds its explanation only in the acceptance by faith of the revealed truth of original sin, is too vast a subject to be discussed here. It seems necessary, however, to consider more closely the structure of that inner order and disorder.

Most difficult to grasp is the fact that it is indeed the essential human self that is capable of throwing itself into disorder to the point of self-destruction. For man is not really a battlefield of conflicting forces and impulses which conquer one another; and if we say that the sensuality "in us" gets the better of our reason, this is only a vague and metaphorical manner of speaking. Rather it is always our single self that is chaste or unchaste, temperate or intemperate, self-preserving or self-destructive. It is always the decisive center of the whole, indivisible person by which the inner order is upheld or upset. "It is not the good my will preserves, but the evil my will disapproves, that *I* find myself doing" (Rom. 7, 19).

Also, the very powers of the human being which most readily appear as the essential powers of self-preservation, self-assertion, and self-fulfillment are at the same time the first to work the opposite: the self-destruction of the moral person. In the *Summa Theologica* we find the almost uncanny formulation: the powers whose ordering is the function of temperance "can most easily bring unrest to the spirit, because they belong to the *essence* of man." [4]

But how can it be that the very powers of self-preservation are so close to becoming destructive? How can it be that the man who seeks himself can miss himself in his very seeking? And how, on the other hand, can self-love be selfless?

A narrow gap of understanding is wedged open by a proposition of St. Thomas's, which may confidently be called the basis of a metaphysical philosophy of active man. It states that to love God more than himself is in accordance with the natural being of man, as of every creature, and with his will as well.[5] Consequently, the offense against the love of God derives its self-destructive sharpness from the fact that it is likewise in conflict with the nature and the natural will of man himself. If he loves nothing so much as himself, man misses and perverts, with inner necessity, the purpose inherent in self-love as in all love: to preserve, to make real, to fulfill. This purpose is given only to selfless self-love, which seeks not itself blindly, but with open eyes endeavors to correspond to the true reality of God, the self, and the world.

The force of this metaphysical truth formulated by Aquinas strikes so deep that, in a sense, it becomes even nonsensical to desire the preservation of the inner order for its own sake and consequently to will even genuine self-preservation as such. (That the *temperantia* of the miser, who shuns debauchery because of its expense, is, as Aquinas says, no virtue, need hardly be mentioned.)[6] It is known how little, for example, a medical directive alone can do to establish true inner discipline; not unjustly has it been said of psychotherapy unrelated to either religion or metaphysics that it tends to produce an "anxiously fostered middle-class tranquillity, poisoned by its triteness,"[7] a result which evidently has nothing to do with the essential serenity of genuine temperance. This failure is no accident, but rather an inevitable consequence. The discipline of temperance cannot be realized with a view to man alone.

The discipline of temperance, understood as selfless self-preservation, is the saving and defending realization of the inner order of man. For temperance not only preserves, it also defends: indeed, it preserves by defending. For since the first sin man has been not only capable of loving himself more than he loves God his Creator but, contrary to his own nature, inclined to do so. The discipline of temperance defends him against all selfish perversion of the inner order, through which alone the moral person exists and lives effectively.

Wherever forces of self-preservation, self-assertion, self-fulfillment, destroy the structure of man's inner being, the discipline of temperance and the license of intemperance enter into play.

The natural urge toward sensual enjoyment, manifested in delight in food and drink and sexual pleasure, is the echo and mirror of man's strongest natural forces of self-preservation. The basic forms of enjoyment correspond to these most primordial forces of being, which tend to preserve the individual man, as well as the whole race, in the existence for which he was created (Wisdom 1, 14). But for the very reason that these forces are closely allied to the deepest human urge toward being, they exceed all other powers of mankind in their destructive violence once they degenerate into selfishness.

Therefore, we find here the actual province of *temperantia*: temperateness and chastity, intemperateness and unchastity, are the primordial forms of the discipline of temperance and the license of intemperance[8] (see Chapters 2, 3).

But we have not, as yet, fully explored the range of the concept of *temperantia.*—In "humility," the instinctive urge to self-assertion can also be made serviceable to genuine self-preservation, but it can likewise pervert and miss this purpose in "pride" [9] (Chapter 7).—And if the natural desire of man to avenge an injustice which he has suffered and to restore his rights explodes in uncontrollable fury, it destroys that which can be preserved only by "gentleness" and "mildness" [10] (Chapter 8). Without rational self-restraint even the natural hunger for sense perception or for knowledge can degenerate into a destructive and pathological compulsive greed; this degradation Aquinas calls *curiositas*, the disciplined mode *studiositas* [11] (Chapter 9).

To sum up: chastity, continence, humility, gentleness, mildness, *studiositas*, are modes of realization of the discipline of temperance; unchastity, incontinence, pride, uninhibited wrath, *curiositas*, are forms of intemperance.

Why is it that one reacts with involuntary irritation to these terms which express the essence of temperance and intemperance, discipline and dissoluteness? Since it can hardly be caused by resistance to the good, this irritation must stem from the thick tangle of misinterpretations which covers and smothers each one of these concepts. This mesh of misinterpretations has its roots in a distortion and falsification of man's ideal image which we can properly term demonic, all the more so since Christians and non-Christians alike regard them as characteristics of the Christian image of man. Worse, the root cause is not just a misconceived image of the good man, but a misconceived view of created reality. *Temperantia* is intimately related to the ordered structure of the being of man, in which all gradations of creation unite; as the history of heresy shows, it is quite particularly in the sphere of *temperantia* that the attitude toward creation and "the world" is most incisively decided.

The attempt to reconstitute the genuine and original meaning of *temperantia* and its various modes of realization must embrace a variety of tasks. It will have to go beyond the strict limits of the subject, in order to anchor the true image of this virtue in the fundamentals of Christian teaching concerning man and reality.

3. Chastity and Unchastity

IN CURRENT TREATISES on chastity and unchastity, the air one breathes is not always bracing.

This state of affairs may have various causes, one of which is certainly this: in contradiction to the true grading and order of things, the realm of sex—again for many different reasons— has moved to the center of attention in the general moral consciousness. In addition to this, and despite all contrary statements of principle, a smoldering subterranean Manichaeism casts suspicion on everything pertaining to physical reproduction as being somehow impure, defiling, and beneath the true dignity of man. From all these and other hidden discords are brewed the oppressive mists of casuistry and distortion, of embarrassment and importunity, which frequently pervade discussions of chastity and unchastity.

On the other hand, it is a refreshing and emancipating experience to read the tractate on the same subject by Aquinas, in his *Summa Theologica*, written with truly holy candor and concise cleanness. Then we realize with joy that we have the right (and more than the right!) to adhere to the principles taught by this "universal teacher" of the Church.

To begin with: for Thomas it is plainly self-evident—indeed so self-evident that it need hardly be mentioned even to those but moderately instructed (while it may still be well not to remain silent on this point)—that the sexual powers are not a "necessary evil" but really a good. With Aristotle, he says incisively that there is something divine in human seed.[1] It is equally self-evident to Thomas's thinking that, "like eating and drinking," the fulfillment of the natural sexual urge and its accompanying pleasure are good and not in the least sinful, assuming, of course, that order and moderation are preserved.[2] For the intrinsic purpose of sexual power, namely, that not only now but also in days to come the children of man may dwell upon the earth and in the Kingdom of God, is not merely a good, but, as Thomas says, "a surpassing good."[3] Indeed, complete asensuality, unfeelingly adverse to all sexual pleasure, which some would like to regard as "properly" perfect and ideal according to Christian doctrine, is described in the *Summa Theologica* not only as an imperfection but actually as a moral defect (*vitium*). [4]

At this point, a deliberate digression is called for. The progenitive purpose of sexuality is not the sole and exclusive purpose of marriage. Yet marriage is the proper fulfillment of sexual power. Of the three goods of marriage—community of life, offspring, and sacramental blessing (*fides, proles, sacramentum*)—it is the mutually benevolent and inviolable community of life which, according to Aquinas, is the special benefit conferred on man "as man." [5]

This affirmative position is clear to Thomas beyond any doubt because, more perhaps than any other Christian teacher, he takes seriously the fundamental thought of revelation, "Everything created by God is good," and thinks it through to its conclusion. These words were used by the Apostle Paul in order to reprimand, with the same reference to creation, those "hypocritical liars" who carry a "torch in their conscience" and "forbid men to marry and to enjoy certain foods" (I Tim. 4, 2f.). Heresy and hyperasceticism are and always have been close neighbors. The Father of the Church, St. John Chrysostom, has expressed this with great emphasis; in a sermon he links the words of Scripture concerning "two in one flesh" to the physical union of the spouses and adds: "Why do you blush? Is it not pure? You are behaving like heretics!" [6]

"The more necessary something is, the more the order of reason must be preserved in it."[7] For the very reason that sexual power is so noble and necessary a good, it needs the preserving and defending order of reason.

Chastity as a virtue, therefore, is constituted in its essence by this and nothing else, namely, that it realizes the order of reason in the province of sexuality.[8] Unchastity as a sin, on the other hand, is in its essence the transgression and violation of the rational order in the province of sexuality. [9]

There is something uncomfortable about the straightforward use of the terms "reason" and "the order of reason" for us modern Christians. But this mistrust, for which, by the way, there is ample cause and reason, must not prevent us from a frank inquiry into what Thomas would have us understand by "reason" and "the order of reason."

Four facts have to be borne in mind if we wish to escape the danger of simply missing St. Thomas's meaning, even before taking a position ourselves. We must consider that Thomas's concept of "reason" and "the order of reason" is to be taken realistically, not idealistically; that it is free of all rationalistic restrictions; that it has none of the connotations of the *ratio* of the Enlightenment; and, finally, that it is not in the least spiritualistic.

The concept "order of reason," first of all, does not signify that something must agree with the imperative of an "absolute reason" detached from its object. *Reason* includes a reference to reality; indeed, it is itself this reference. "In accord with reason" is in this sense that which is right "in itself," that which corresponds to reality itself.[10] The order of reason accordingly signifies that something is disposed in accordance with the truth of real things.

Secondly, *ratio* is not that reason which arbitrarily restricts itself to the province of purely natural cognition. *Ratio* here signifies—in its widest sense—man's power to grasp reality. Now, man grasps reality not only in natural cognition but also —and this reality is a higher object of knowledge and the process of grasping it a higher process—by faith in the revelation of God. If therefore the *Summa Theologica* states that Christ is the chief Lord (*principalis Dominus*), the first owner of our bodies, and that one who uses his body in a manner contrary to order, injures Christ the Lord Himself,[11] Thomas is not of the opinion that this proposition exceeds[12] the pattern of "mere" rational order, but rather that for Christian thought to be guided by divine revelation is the very highest form of "accord with reason"—this in spite of the fact that elsewhere Thomas knows how to distinguish sharply between natural and supernatural cognition. "The order of reason," accordingly, is the order which corresponds to the reality made evident to man through faith and knowledge.

Thirdly, the emphatic and ever recurrent stress on reason and the order of reason in works of Aquinas is obviously not to be understood in the sense which the Enlightenment has given to these terms. "To realize the order of reason in the province of sexuality" is a proposition which one most certainly would not want to understand as an incitement or permission to lift that which natural feeling and propriety surround and protect with the sheltering obscurity of concealment and silence into the crude and artificial light of a shallow "know-it-all" view. Rather, Thomas expressly co-ordinates modesty with chastity, whose function is to see to it that this silence and this obscurity are not destroyed either by shamelessness or uninhibited rationalizing, or spotlighted by the methods of "sexual instruction."[13] This, therefore, forms part of the "order of reason" too.

Fourthly, the Thomistic concept of reason might be misinterpreted spiritualistically, a facile temptation to some. The proposition that "the essential and proper good of man is existence in accord with reason"[14] could be read to mean: "Constant spiritual awareness is what distinguishes the specifically human condition; everything that clouds this awareness is unspiritual, consequently unworthy of the human condition, and therefore evil." Applied to the province here under discussion such a spiritualistic interpretation might easily lead to the following conclusion: "In the act of procreation, reason is so overwhelmed by the abundance of pleasure that, as the philosopher says, spiritual cognition becomes impossible . . . ; thus there can be no act of begetting without sin." Now this last sentence is actually to be found in the *Summa Theologica* of St. Thomas—but as an "objection," that is, as an expressly confuted opinion, as a negation to which a clear affirmation is opposed. The affirmation is worded as follows: "As long as the sexual act itself corresponds to the rational order, the abundance of pleasure does not conflict with the proper mean of virtue. . . . And even the fact that reason is unable to make a free act of cognition of spiritual things simultaneously with that pleasure does not prove that the sexual act conflicts with virtue. For it is not against virtue that the workings of reason sometimes are interrupted by something that takes place in accordance with reason: otherwise it would be contrary to virtue to sleep."[15] Do we need any further explanation in order to show how much St. Thomas's concept of reason has regard to the *whole* man—to body and soul, sensuality and spirituality? St. Thomas designates as "not in accord with reason" the opinion of some Fathers of the Church that "in Paradise the propagation of mankind would have taken place in some other manner, such as that of the angels";[16] indeed, St. Thomas says: The pleasure that accompanies intercourse must have been even stronger in Paradise—since mental awareness was unclouded and because of the greater delicacy of human nature and the higher sensitivity of the body.[17] But enough of this.

Only on the basis of these four delimitations and refutations is our vision liberated so that we can see the true core of the proposition that chastity, by disciplining sexuality, realizes the order of reason.

The order of reason, however, implies, first, that the immanent purpose of sexual power be not perverted but fulfilled (in marriage, with its threefold "good"); second, that the inner structure of the moral person be kept intact; and, third, that justice between men be not infringed. What we are concerned with here is the purpose of sex as it was intended originally in the first creation, and ennobled by Christ in the New Creation; what we are concerned with is the existential structure of the moral person, as established in nature and in grace; what we are concerned with is order among men as guaranteed not merely by natural justice, but also by the higher justice of *caritas*, that is, supernatural love of God and man.

Chastity realizes in the province of sex the order which corresponds to the truth of the world and of man both as experienced and as revealed, and which accords with the twofold form of this truth—not that of unveiled evidence alone, but that of veiled evidence also—that is, of mystery.

It is not adultery only which touches upon the provinces of both *temperantia* and justice;[18] rather, any unchastity has these two aspects: to be at once intemperance and injustice. St. Thomas relates the totality of all sins against chastity to the "common weal"—taking this term in a very profound and far-reaching sense—and to justice as well;[19] similarly, he relates all the Ten Commandments, not excepting the sixth and the ninth, to justice.[20]

We have become used to see in adultery, and even more in adulterous desire and cupidity, as in sexual transgressions generally, almost exclusively the element of lust, neglecting almost completely the element of injustice. Yet it is very important that the collective moral consciousness of Christianity should again assign greater weight to this objective side of chastity, which is concerned with the common weal and with justice, as against a view limited exclusively to the subjective factor. To restore the proper emphasis is evidently important not only because it corresponds to actual fact and truth, but also because the neglect or insufficient observation of the objective element of justice in chastity and its opposite derives from an erroneous conception of man and at the same time causes and perpetuates this error.

In this book, which treats of *temperantia* and not of the sixth commandment nor of marriage nor of the Christian idea of man as a whole, nor of justice, it is quite enough that this thought has been given emphatic expression.

Here, however, it is our purpose to consider chastity and unchastity expressly from the point of view of moderation and its opposite, being fully aware, at the same time, of the limitations inherent in the subject. We shall speak first not of its outward repercussions, but of its root in the inner man: of the disciplining of the sex urge by the spiritual directing power of reason, and also of the abdication of the spirit, which opens the way for sex to destroy the moral person.

In what way and why does unchastity destroy the structure of the person?

Unchastity most effectively falsifies and corrupts the virtue of prudence.[21] All that conflicts with the virtue of prudence stems for the most part from unchastity;[22] unchastity begets a blindness of spirit which practically excludes all understanding of the goods of the spirit;[23] unchastity splits the power of decision;[24] conversely, the virtue of chastity more than any other makes man capable and ready for contemplation.[25]

All these propositions of St. Thomas do not refer to isolated effects and consequences; if the spirit is blinded by unchastity, it is not by a process similar to the wilting of a plant in a rainless period. This blindness is of the essence of unchastity itself, which is by its very nature destructive. It is not its outward effect and consequence, but its immanent essential property.

"The being of man in its essential significance consists in this: to be in accord with reason. If therefore a man keeps to what is in accord with reason, he is said 'to keep himself in himself.'"[26] Unchastity destroys in a very special manner this self-possession and this human "keeping of oneself in oneself." Unchaste abandon and the self-surrender of the soul to the world of sensuality paralyzes the primordial powers of the moral person: the ability to perceive, in silence, the call of reality, and to make, in the retreat of this silence, the decision appropriate to the concrete situation of concrete action. This is the meaning inherent in all those propositions which speak of the falsification and corruption of prudence, of the blindness of the spirit, and of the splitting of the power of decision.

Now all this is not to be understood as if the corruptive effect of unchastity derived from the fact that the spirit turns to the "sensual" and "inferior" in general. On the contrary, such turning is altogether inevitable for any decision. It is indeed of the essence of the virtue of prudence that it face squarely all those concrete realities which surround man's concrete actions. Accordingly, it is not the reference to the province of sexuality that produces the blindness and deafness brought about by unchastity; such an opinion would be Manichaean at bottom, and therefore anti-Christian.

Rather, the destructiveness lies in the fact that unchastity constricts man and thus renders him incapable of seeing objective reality. An unchaste man wants above all something for himself; he is distracted by an unobjective "interest"; his constantly strained will-to-pleasure prevents him from confronting reality with that selfless detachment which alone makes genuine knowledge possible. St. Thomas here uses the comparison of a lion who, at the sight of a stag, is unable to perceive anything but the anticipated meal. In an unchaste heart, attention is not merely fixed upon a certain track, but the "window" of the soul has lost its "transparency," that is, its capacity for perceiving existence, as if a selfish interest had covered it, as it were, with a film of dust. (We cannot repeat too often: only he who is silent hears, only the invisible is transparent.)

This kind of interestedness is altogether selfish. The abandonment of an unchaste heart to the sensual world has nothing in common with the genuine dedication of a searcher for truth to the reality of being, of a lover to his beloved. Unchastity does not dedicate itself, it offers itself. It is selfishly intent upon the "prize," upon the reward of illicit lust. "Chaste," says St. Augustine, "is the heart that loves God without looking for reward."[27] One further comment: For anyone whose function it is to lead and counsel young people, it is extremely important to keep in mind and to make known that it is this selfishness which characterizes the inner nature of unchastity (as intemperance). Where the selfish motive is absent, we may speak of thoughtlessness, curiosity, or of impulses so completely natural that they lie outside the scope of moral judgment—but not of unchastity.

This perversion of a genuine process of knowing is all the more destructive the more immediately a given knowledge concerns man himself and the more it can be the foundation of moral decisions.[28] Not only is the cognitive process thereby poisoned and perverted, but also the power of decision itself, and even more so; "most of all prudence," says Aquinas.[29] It is prudence, however, which, as the perfection of conscience, is the innermost source-region of the moral person. Prudence implies a transformation of the knowledge of truth into decisions corresponding to reality. This transformation is achieved in three steps: deliberation, judgment, decision.[30] Upon each of these three steps the destructive power of intemperance manifests itself: in place of deliberation guided by the truth of things, we find complete recklessness and inconsideration; a hasty judgment that will not wait until reason has weighed the pros and cons; and even if a correct decision were reached, it would always be endangered by the fickleness of a heart that abandons itself indiscriminately to the surging mass of sensual impressions.[31] This is inevitable: if you do not move a knife in the plane of the thing to be cut, it cannot cut at all. So without a direct, innocent, and selfless vision of reality there can be no interior order of the moral person and no honest moral decision.

Chastity, on the other hand, renders one able to perceive reality and ready not only for the perception and thus also for decision corresponding to reality, but also for that highest mode of relating oneself to reality in which the purest dedication to knowledge and the most selfless dedication in love become one, namely, contemplation, in which man turns toward the divine Being and becomes aware of that truth which is at once the highest good.

To be open to the truth of real things and to live by the truth that one has grasped is the essence of the moral being. Only when we recognize this state of things can we likewise understand the depths to which the unchaste heart permits destruction to invade its very being.

This dark portrayal of the destructive force of unchastity applies in all its harshness only to unchastity as *intemperantia*, but not to unchastity as *incontinentia*; just as that which has been said of chastity is fully pertinent only to chastity as *temperantia* but not to chastity as *continentia*.[32] This significant distinction must be briefly explained.

Because it *is* not always the same thing when two people *do* the same thing, a moral doctrine which regards only the actions of man but not his being, is always in danger of seeing only the sameness (or the difference) of the actions, and missing important differences (or samenesses) at a greater depth. Since, however, the moral theology of the universal teacher of the Church is a doctrine of virtue—that is, a doctrine of the *being* of man as the source of his actions—the difference between *temperantia-intemperantia* on the one hand and *continentia-incontinentia* on the other hand could not easily escape him.

Chastity as *temperantia*, or unchastity as *intemperantia*: This means that each, respectively, has become a deep-rooted basic attitude of man, and, as it were, a second nature to him. Chastity as *continentia*, or unchastity as *incontinentia*: This means that neither is necessarily based on what might be called a natural inclination of being; neither has as yet grown firm roots in the existential core of man. This second mode of chastity is not the perfected virtue of temperance and moderation, but a strenuous control; and this mode of unchastity is not a consummate intemperance, but a mere lack of control. Chastity as control is only a tentative sketch; chastity as *temperantia* is perfected realization. The first is less perfect than the second, because by the former, the directing power of reason has been able to mold only the conscious will, but not yet the sensual urge, whereas by the latter will and urge are both stamped with "rational order".[33] In Thomas's explicit opinion, the effort of self-control pertains only to the less perfect steps of the beginner, whereas real, perfected virtue, by the very nature of its concept, bears the joyous, radiant seal of ease, of effortlessness, of self-evident inclination.[34] On the other hand, unchastity in the form of lack of self-control is less pernicious, less sinful, than unchastity in the form of actual intemperance. In the first case, as Aristotle[35] and St. Thomas[36] say, the best is not lost; the principle, the ground of being, subsists, namely, the right conception of the direction of will toward the true goal; and through this unblemished rightness even the sensual urge can be reintegrated again and again into its order: he who sins from lack of control is quick to repent;[37] and repentance is the repudiation of sin. On the other hand, he who sins from a deep-rooted basic attitude of intemperance directs his will expressly toward sin; he does not repent easily; indeed, "he is happy to have sinned, because sinning has become 'natural' for him."[38] The merely uncontrolled can be "recalled" to order; actual intemperance, however, is not easily revocable.[39] To sin from a basic attitude of one's will is real malice; to sin in a gust of passion is weakness—*infirmitas.*[40] One who is merely uncontrolled *is* not unchaste, even though he *acts* unchastely.[41]

It is no doubt easy to see that to stress this difference is not to indulge in the pleasure of theoretical hair-splitting. Rather, it is an attempt to establish a contrast which acquires an immediately practical significance, both pedagogical and pastoral.

It is *temperantia,* the virtue that realizes the inner order of man in himself, which St. Thomas has in mind when—in contrast to justice, in whose province that which is "properly and in itself right" can and must be determined—speaking of "the other moral virtues which refer to the passions and in which right or wrong cannot be determined in the same fashion, because men vary in their attitudes toward the passions," he says, "therefore it is necessary that what is right and reasonable in the passions should be determined with reference to *ourselves,* who are moved by the passions."[42] But especially in the province of *temperantia* "we ourselves" have the choice of innumerable possibilities: for example, to desire halfheartedly or wholeheartedly, to tolerate, to let things take their course, to give in to pressure or to be carried away. "Who could determine," writes the perceptive Thomist, H. D. Noble, in his commentary on the French edition of Aquinas—[43]"who could determine when lack of control ends and when actual intemperance begins?"

St. Thomas says that the realization of *temperantia* varies too much according to individuals and periods to allow the establishment of hard and fast, universally valid commandments on *temperantia*.[44] The whole realm of "unchaste thoughts, desires, words, looks, etc.," which in the casuistic manuals occupies so much space, is treated in the *Summa Theologica* in a single article not quite one page in length. It determines the general principle only, that it is not the accomplished sinful act alone that is sinful, but also the willing consent to the pleasure imagined and implicit in this act; for this willing consent is inconceivable without an attitude of acceptance toward the accomplished act itself;[45] everything, therefore, which derives from such willing consent is likewise a sin.[46]

Within this frame of reference it should certainly be possible to construe, after the manner of the casuist, a series of typical "individual cases" exemplifying the springs of action, a simplified and meaningful "scheme" of human behavior. But how are we to react to a proposition such as this one, found in one of the most popular handbooks of moral theology: "To look at the private parts of animals out of curiosity, but without voluptuousness . . . is a venial sin"? Not to mention other distortions,[47] it seems that here the limit beyond which casuistry becomes meaningless has been considerably exceeded. Propositions so constructed seem entirely to miss the true purpose and scope of casuistry, which is to provide a tentative approach and an auxiliary means for the practice of discernment. Is it not to be feared that a discernment schooled by such methods will be misguided toward an unrealistic rigidity and a prematurely fixed judgment, instead of toward a sober evaluation of the realities of life; and that this in turn may lead to a total incomprehension of the reality of man as a being who responds to the richly orchestrated world with every power of his soul, and thus reaches his choice?

We have spoken of the destructive power of unchastity and of the preserving, perfecting, fulfilling power of chastity. Something more must be added to this subject.

Without chastity, not only is the satiation of the spirit with truth rendered impossible, but also actual sensual joy in what is sensually beautiful. That Christian doctrine does not exclude sensual enjoyment from the realm of the morally good (as against the merely "permissible") does not need to be specifically stated. But that this enjoyment should be made possible only by the virtue of temperance and moderation—that, indeed, is a surprising thought. Yet this is what we read in the *Summa Theologica*, in the first question of the tractate on temperance[48]—even if more between and behind the lines than in what is said directly. In the case of animals, it is said there, no pleasure is derived from the activity of the other senses, such as the eye and the ear, except as they affect the satisfaction of the drives of hunger and sex; only because of the promise of food is the lion "happy" when he spies a stag or hears his call. Man, by contrast, is able to enjoy what is seen or heard for the sensual "appropriateness" alone which appeals to the eye and the ear—by this, nothing else but sensual beauty is to be understood.[49] One frequently reads and hears that in intemperance man sinks to the level of the beast—a dictum to be used with caution, for intemperance (like temperance) is something exclusively human; neither angel nor animal can know it. But keeping this distinction in mind, the sentence becomes meaningful: unchaste lust has the tendency to relate the whole complex of the sensual world, and particularly of sensual beauty, to sexual pleasure exclusively. Therefore only a chaste sensuality can realize the specifically human faculty of perceiving sensual beauty, such as that of the human body, as beauty, and to enjoy it for its own sake, for its "sensual appropriateness," undeterred and unsullied by the self-centered will to pleasure. It has been said that only the pure of heart can laugh freely and liberatingly. It is no less true that only those who look at the world with pure eyes can experience its beauty.

Unlike all other virtues, it has always been the strange fate of the virtue of temperance and moderation, especially in its aspect of chastity, not to be valued and practiced or scorned and ridiculed more or less at its face value, but to be overestimated and overvalued in a very specific sense. This is something altogether unique. There have, of course, always been theoretical discussions about the hierarchy of the virtues, and one or the other has been shifted to a higher rank. But the stubborn and really quite fanatical preference given to *temperantia*, especially to chastity, which runs through the whole history of Christian doctrine as a more or less hidden undercurrent or countercurrent, has a very special aspect. No one, at any rate, has attached to justice or prudence or to any of the three theological virtues such an emphatic and evidently not simply factual, but emotionally charged, evaluation.

Of course, there would not be the slightest objection against such an evaluation *per se*—for strictly speaking, virtues as such cannot be overrated. But here we are speaking of an evaluation and overevaluation based on a false premise; of an evaluation, therefore, which implies a misunderstanding of what is supposedly valued so highly. And against this we must object strongly.

In the province of *temperantia*, as we have said before, it is man's attitude toward creation which is decided, and most incisively. And the "wrong premise" upon which rest the overevaluation and erroneous value given to *temperantia* in general and chastity in particular amounts to this, namely, the explicit or implied opinion that the sensual reality of the whole of creation, and above all the nonspiritual element in man himself, is actually evil. To sum up: the "wrong premise" is an explicit, or, more often, an implicit, even unconscious and unintended, Manichaeism.

That man must eat, that he must sleep, that the origin of new human life is linked to the physical union of man and woman—all this, especially the last, appears, in this presumably ineradicable apprehension of the world, as a necessary evil—perhaps not even a necessary one—something unworthy of God the Creator and of man as well. The specifically human task, or better still, the specifically Christian task, would consist in rising above this entire "lower" sphere and mounting by ascetic practice to a purely spiritual way of life. Not only do fasting, vigils, and sexual continence take on a very special importance from this basic approach, but they move necessarily into the center of attention of the man striving for perfection. This evaluation, however, shares and indeed intensifies the errors of its origin; and despite all outward similarity, it has as little to do with the Christian evaluation of those three things as the heresies of the Manichees, the Montanists, and the Cathari have to do with the Catholic dogma that proclaims that created reality is good in all its spheres, and is not subject to the arbitrariness of human evaluation; indeed, it is the basis and the point of departure of all evaluation as well as of all realization of value. [50]

That "wrong premise" with its effects on ethical doctrine is particularly evident in the Montanist writings of Tertullian, who, by reason of his ambiguous status as a quasi-Father of the Church (St. Thomas speaks of him only as a heretic: *haereticus, Tertullianus nomine*),[51] has continued to this day as the ancestor and the chief witness of that erroneous evaluation of *temperantia.* One need only enumerate the subjects of his works: "On Modesty," "On the Veiling of Virgins," "On the Adornment of Women," "On Fasting," "Admonition to Chastity," "Concerning Stage Plays," or mention his rejection of second marriages after the death of wife or husband, in order to show that the realm of *temperantia* is very prominently under scrutiny. For Tertullian, unchastity is to such a point the primal form of sin that according to him the sin of the angels was unchastity, and thus they fell from God; this is what he thought St. Paul had in mind when he said that women should veil themselves "because of the angels" (I Cor. 4, 10).[52] To the same frame of reference belongs the cause of Tertullian's separation from the Church only a few years after his baptism: he could neither comprehend nor condone the fact that Pope Callistus welcomed back into the ecclesiastical community those sinners against chastity who had done the required penance contritely. Tertullian denounces the encyclical with which the Pope proclaims this measure as a blot upon the Church, fit to be read "in those dens of vice, beneath the signboards of the whorehouses rather than in the house of God."[53] It is characteristic, also, that already with Tertullian the emphasis on external action appears which customarily and as if from inner necessity accompanies the erroneous evaluation of *temperantia,* and more especially of chastity: he calls for more obligatory fast days; for the veiling of women and girls; and he sees the hallmark of a Christian in his abstention from public entertainments.[54]

Blindness only can deny that this Manichaean undervaluation of the sensual reality of creation (let us repeat: not as a formulated opinion, but as an inarticulate attitude) tinges and surreptitiously qualifies the current Christian notion of the virtue of temperance, and more especially of chastity. This becomes evident in innumerable small traits pertaining to the thinking and speaking habits of Christian folk, and also not infrequently in the accents and shadings of moral preaching itself.

If, for example, one speaks with special emphasis of the defilement of unchastity, this implies a different and weightier blame than the defilement pertaining to any other sin. (Actually, the term "defilement" is almost never applied to other sins.) What is censured is not only the specific "vulgarity" inherent in any form of self-indulging pleasure; there is also almost always a persistently audible undertone suggesting the idea of contact with something in itself impure, with a reality defiling *per se*. The current notion of the "Immaculate Conception"—current even among Christians—refers this immaculateness not so much to the person of the Virgin Mary as to the process of conception, of begetting (and often enough, as anyone can test, not to the conception of Mary, but to that of the Lord in the womb of His mother). Among people generally, this immaculateness is in any case not understood as it is understood by the Church and by theology, namely, as signifying that Mary was free from the stain of original sin from her mother's womb. The current popular notion, rather, is this: by a special grace of God, that conception remained free from the impurity and taint which naturally adheres to it, as to all begetting and conception. And even if this immaculateness is correctly referred to the person of the Virgin Mary herself, as in the appellation Mary "Immaculate," we find on close listening that the concept has been totally deprived of its universal, inclusive significance, and has been limited to the province of chastity alone.—Something similar is true of the concept of purity, which, also viewed Biblically, is much broader in scope than chastity. For the average understanding it has become entirely natural to refer the beatitude "Blessed are the pure in heart" exclusively, or at any rate principally, to chastity, though neither the immediate Biblical meaning nor the interpretation of these words of the Lord in classical theology favors such restriction; Aquinas, for example, by no means assigns the beatitude of the pure in heart to the virtue of chastity, but to the supernatural virtue of faith.[55]—Finally: Try to ascertain what the average Christian associates with the sentence: To the pure all things are pure. First, he will not readily imagine that this phrase is to be found in the New Testament (Titus 1, 15) and that it only affirms what was said by Jesus Himself (Matt. 15, 10-20); on the contrary, the average Christian, such as we find him in every walk of life and on every educational level, would sooner have guessed at a non-Christian, liberal author. And it is scarcely ever thought of that aside from and indeed predating its misused liberal interpretation, this sentence has a sound and important Christian significance. Of course here again purity is confined to chastity, in evident contradiction to the sense of the context.[56] And since the presumably Christian sense of the Biblical sentence is supposed to imply that even to the pure man *not* everything is pure, we find here again the effects of the notion of the essential impurity of the reality of being.

These misconceptions, which miss the actual Christian meaning of things—and examples of which could be multiplied—can only be partially attributed to ignorance. They propagate themselves, in the form of inarticulate opinions and attitudes, beneath and beyond and even in spite of formal instruction; as a rule, the average Christian we here have in mind will, after some concentration on the relevant article in his catechism, be able to give the "theoretically" correct answer. Decisive, however, are not so much the explicit words as the atmosphere in the province of moral education and teaching; and it must be admitted by even the most cautious judgment that this atmosphere is plainly not entirely free from the germs of Manichaeism. And no cleansing can be effected by mere theoretical knowledge and cognition, or by instruction only. What is required is that the dogmatic truth of God the Creator and His works be wholly appropriated in humbly confident assent, and that this truth obtain the radiant and vivifying power which is the exclusive property of genuine vitality.

But the "world" exists not only as God's creation. There is also the "world" which, as St. John the Apostle says, "lies in evil" and prevails in the "gratification of corrupt nature, gratification of the eyes, and the empty pomp of living" (I John 22, 16); there is the kingdom of the "Prince of this world" (John 12, 31, Luke 4, 6); there is the world for which Christ the Lord did not want to pray (John 17, 9). There is not only the reality of creation, but also the perversion of the order of creation, which has taken on form in the activities of men and the objective "creations" which grow out of these. And this "world" also comes up for judgment in the sphere of *temperantia*, in a very specific sense. It is in that which aids and abets the self-indulging lust for pleasure that the inversion of the order of creation may most obtrusively be realized, filling the foreground of the "world" completely with its seductive call. (Though of course the core and substance of that world which lies in evil consists primarily in the realization of injustice and above all in the actual denial of faith, hope, and charity—a telling counterpart to the hierarchy of the virtues!) From this point of view the evaluation and educational emphasis put on the virtue of temperance rightly achieves special significance. This sort of estimate of *temperantia*, however, has to be carefully distinguished from the previously mentioned "Manichaean" variety (not always an easy task, as the Manichaeans constantly adduce the valid arguments of the other side together with their own). Even the rigorist attitude of the Carthaginian Tertullian is partially conditioned by his constant experience of metropolitan life. "It is bad to live in cities: there are too many lecherous people," reads the beginning of the chapter on chastity in Nietzsche's *Zarathustra*. What Nietzsche asserts with hard-hitting precision was also known to Thomas, who formulates it more dispassionately and ab-

stractly: "There is not much sinning because of natural desires.
. . . But the stimuli of desire which man's cunning has de-
vised are something else, and for the sake of these one sins very
much."[57] Intemperance is enkindled above all by the seductive
glamour of the stimuli provided in an artificial civilization,
with which the dishonorable team of blind lust and calculated
greed surround the province of sexuality. All training and self-
discipline aiming at chastity will find itself constantly faced
with this situation. The resulting "overemphasis" on *temperantia* is in a certain sense fully justified (even though, on the
other hand, the ethics of the so-called "fight against public
immorality" seem to be a precarious and debatable business—
and not only because of their ineffectiveness). Even St.
Thomas assigns to *temperantia* primacy before fortitude and
justice—though in a circumscribed, nonactual sense—since it
must be most often proven in the world.[58] We say in a circumscribed, nonactual sense, for the hierarchy which is actually
and essentially valid is of a different kind.

But first a comment is necessary to avoid facile misunder-
standings. In these considerations it is not a question of mini-
mizing the gravity of the sins against chastity. No attempt at
palliation can lessen the fearful weight of the willful turning of
man from God. But we must never lose sight of the fact that
the essential nature of sin lies exclusively in this willful turning
away from God.[59] On the other hand, the opinion (again
founded on Tertullian) that unchastity is the gravest of all
sins,[60] seems to base the gravity of this sin not so much on the
turning away from God as on the turning of man to the goods
of the sensual world; or, more directly and revealingly expressed: on defilement by a reality presumed to be impure and
evil in its essence. St. Thomas, however, states that even a
disordered turning of man to a transitory good, if it does not
include a turning away from God, cannot be a mortal sin.[61]
But even the *Summa* once quotes the sentence of St. Isidore

of Seville according to which the human race succumbs to the devil more through unchastity than in any other way.[62] In the moral teaching of the last hundred years this thought has played a dominant role, to an extent where it is overrefined to a definiteness of statement exceeding all human competence. How could a mere human being be able to know that—as a widely read theological writer of our times asserts—"there are ninety-nine people out of a hundred who will be damned for this very sin!"[63] For St. Thomas, by contrast, the proposition of St. Isidore merely proved that in the sin of unchastity the compelling force of sensual desire is most effective; this very fact, however, mitigates the gravity of the sin, "because the sin is more venial the more overwhelming the sensual passion that drives one to it."[64]

But let us return to the consideration of the hierarchy of the virtues and the place of *temperantia* in that hierarchy. Over and over again Thomas has raised the question of the hierarchy of the virtues. His reply is as follows: "Man's good is rational good. But this good is possessed in its essence by prudence, which is the perfection of reason. But justice is the agent which makes this good real. It is the portion of justice to establish in all human affairs the order of reason. But the other virtues maintain and protect this good, insofar as they order the passions, lest these turn man away from rational good. In the hierarchy of these virtues fortitude has the first place. It is followed by temperance. That which concerns being is higher than that which concerns operation; and this again is higher than that which concerns maintenance and protection, inasmuch as only that which hinders is removed. Consequently, among the cardinal virtues prudence is the noblest; justice is the second, fortitude the third, *temperantia* the fourth."[65] "Justice and fortitude are higher virtues than temperance; but they are all exceeded by prudence and the theological virtues."[66]

Temperantia in its strict and ultimate sense is not "realization" of the good.[67] Discipline, moderation, chastity, do not in themselves constitute the perfection of man. By preserving and defending order in man himself, *temperantia* creates the indispensable prerequisite for both the realization of actual good and the actual movement of man toward his goal. Without it, the stream of the innermost human will-to-be would overflow destructively beyond all bounds, it would lose its direction and never reach the sea of perfection. Yet *temperantia* is not itself the stream. But it is the shore, the banks, from whose solidity the stream receives the gift of straight unhindered course, of force, descent, and velocity.

4. Virginity

THE NOBLE, truly princely practice of spending lavishly in order to make splendidly visible some sublime thought —either in a solemn celebration, in sculpture, or in architecture—this virtue (for it is a virtue!) the Middle Ages called *magnificentia.* We no longer can describe it in a single word. But the relation of *magnificentia* to ordinary generosity, which belongs to the daily sphere of needs and requests, is the same, says St. Thomas, as the relation of virginity to chastity.[1]

One might almost say that we lack today the right word for virginity also. For "virginity" designates in popular parlance the condition of intactness and singleness rather than the virtue, born of grace and resolve, of him who for the sake of God has forever renounced the experience of sexual enjoyment. Again we are constrained to think that this poverty of language must have its deepest cause in the fact that the popular mind is no longer deeply aware of the thing itself. However that may be, if here we briefly expound the nature of the virtue of *virginitas* under the name of virginity, we needs must keep in mind many discrepancies from current usages of speech and interpretation.

First: Virginity is not a fact, but an act; not a condition, but a decision. That which constitutes virginity as a virtue is not mere inviolateness as a psychic (and certainly not as a physical) factor, even though this inviolateness may be the trophy of heroic chastity. Virginity as a virtue is established by the decision, or, to speak even more accurately, by the vow to refrain forever from sexual union and its attendant pleasure.

Nor is this all. Such a decision might spring from all sorts of reasons, for instance, from the anti-Christian view that this kind of abstinence is nothing but abstinence from evil.—Two things are involved in this decision, or rather enter into it and pervade it utterly.

First: "Virginity is honored not because it is virginity, but because it is consecrated."[2] The decision to live in sexual abstinence is not in itself worthy of praise; it is "made praiseworthy only by its end and purpose, to the extent that it aims to make him who practises it free for things divine."[3] It would be well if not only the non-Christian but the Christian also always kept in mind these two incontrovertible sentences of the greatest teachers of the Church, St. Augustine and St. Thomas, and remembered that consequently a virginity which does not realize the purpose of being free for God and for divine things becomes correspondingly meaningless and, in any case, loses the dignity for which it is honored by the Church. Of course, various chance necessities or even moral reasons may force or move a man to remain unmarried; and evidently the radiance of a sacrifice offered to God can be imparted to such a necessity or choice. But to prize, on purely religious grounds, a celibacy that lacks the support of its most essential foundation, necessarily borders on Manichaeism, which regards the bare fact of celibacy itself as a good—and consequently sees something evil in marriage.

And here we come to the second fact expressed in the Christian decision to remain virginal: the affirmation of marriage as both a natural and a supernatural good. The Church has expressed this affirmation not only "where it belongs," that is, not only in the liturgy of the Nuptial Mass and in dogmatic decisions concerning the seventh sacrament. It is affirmed in the very prayer at the consecration of virgins, where she speaks of the sanctity of matrimony and of the blessing that rests upon it; and in this very place virginity is expressly related to the same mystery that is included in the matrimonial union of man and wife.[4]

Only because of this mystery of the union with Christ, only because it fosters a more undivided devotion to God, is virginity superior to marriage. That virginity, chosen for the sake of a positive goal, really makes possible a fuller concentration need not be further discussed; it is evident to everybody that soldiers and political leaders remain freer for their tasks if they stay single.

On the other hand, however, we have the words of St. Catherine of Genoa, to a priest who spoke of the higher sanctity of the celibate life to her, who was a wife and a mother: Not even life in a military camp could distract her from her love of God—how much less, marriage! "If world or husband could hinder love, what a petty thing love would be!"[5]—With these refreshingly outspoken words the saint names not only the ultimate and decisive foundation of all sanctity (which, as St. Thomas teaches,[6] is not virginity, but love of God) but she also rightfully objects to the contrasting of the married and the virginal person (*in concreto*) as beings of different value, instead of the contrasting (*in abstracto*) of marriage and virginity. "Better the chastity of celibates than the chastity of the married; but I, the celibate, am not better than Abraham," says St. Augustine.[7] And in his book on virginity he admonishes virgins consecrated to God: "Whence does the virgin know, no matter how she may seek what is the Lord's, whether perhaps, for some weakness unknown to her, she is not yet ripe for the trial of martyrdom; and whether that married woman to whom she thinks herself superior may not already be able to drink the chalice of the Lord's suffering!"[8]

There are two, as it were, eternal objections to virginity: first, that it is against nature, and second, that by weakening the generative power of the people, it conflicts with the common weal. Only those ignorant of the range and acumen of St. Thomas's mind will be surprised to find both objections most precisely formulated in the *Summa Theologica*.[9]

More important still is his reply, built up in a three-membered argument.

First, the objection: As it is natural that man should give up his external goods—money and property—for the sake of his bodily health, so it is not contrary to nature that man renounce the gratification of physical desire for the sake of his spiritual and intellectual life. This is the natural order, appropriate to the nature of things and of man.—But how is this? No one would stop eating and drinking for the sake of spiritual goods, and is it not said in Holy Scripture: "Increase and multiply and people the earth!" (Gen. 1, 28).

Second, the answer: There are two kinds of natural *must* and *may*: one is for the individual *I*, the other for the community of the *we*. Each individual *must* eat and drink. But the command of Genesis applies to the whole community of mankind. "In the army some keep watch over the camp, others are standard-bearers, and others fight with the sword. All these things are duties which make for community life which, in turn, cannot be carried out by the individual." It is consequently necessary for the human community "not only that it be propagated, but also that it flourish spiritually and intellectually. And therefore the common human weal has received its due if some fulfill the function of physical generation, while others, refraining from this, are entirely liberated for the contemplation of things divine—for the beauty and the salvation of the whole of mankind." [10]

Third, to clinch the argument: "The common weal is higher than the individual's, if both are of the same kind; but it may be that the good of the individual is of a higher kind. In this way virginity consecrated to God ranks higher than physical fertility."[11]

There are certain concepts which, as in a concave mirror, draw together a complete view of the world. And these same concepts are the crossroads where minds either meet or part. Of such is the concept of virginity.

Only he who recognizes the hierarchy which informs the three-membered argument of St. Thomas—namely, that the divine is infinitely higher than the human, and that the spiritual towers above the physical—who recognizes this hierarchy not only "conceptually" but "really" (to speak with Newman), he alone can comprehend the significance, the justification, and the dignity of virginity.

The notion and the actuality of the virginal life dedicated to God rise up like a sign of challenge. In this sign it becomes manifest whether the intellectual and spiritual goods really, validly, and vitally occupy their appropriate place and rank. In this sign also it becomes manifest whether these goods are counted among those by virtue of which the community of the people lives—"for the beauty and salvation of the whole of mankind."

5. On Fasting

HILARITAS MENTIS—cheerfulness of heart. Christian dogma links this notion most closely to the primal form of all asceticism, fasting.[1] This connection is based on the New Testament, on the Lord's admonition, proclaimed by the Church every year at the beginning of Lent: "When you fast, do not shew it by gloomy looks!" (Matt. 6, 16).

St. Augustine says that it is a matter of indifference what or how much a man eats, provided the welfare of those with whom he is associated, his own welfare and the requirements of health be not disregarded; what matters, he says, is just one thing, namely, the ease and cheerfulness of heart with which he is able to renounce food if necessity or moral obligation require it. [2]

If necessity demands. This needs no elaboration. But what about fasting as a moral obligation? The reply leads us to the heart of the matter, and to a point of information that may greatly surprise modern Christians. We are inclined and accustomed to see in the practice of fasting a traditional and surely very meaningful custom of the Church; a custom which has somehow gathered obligatory force, but only by virtue of a purely disciplinary regulation of the Church, which is clearly ready to grant all kinds of alleviations and dispensations. Otherwise, fasting seems to us something extraordinary in every sense, linked at once to the idea of the ascetic and the saint. It is with some surprise, therefore, that we read in Aquinas, the "universal teacher" of the Church, that fasting is a commandment of the natural law, quite specifically intended for the average Christian.[3] At this point it is important to recall that for St. Thomas the "natural law" is the fundamental source of obligation. The natural moral law is the ultimate "ought," given and established directly in the nature of created reality, and as such endowed with supreme binding power. Consequently, the fasting regulations of the Church go back to this fundamental obligation, and constitute only a more accurately defined form, modified according to temporal circumstances and prevailing customs. [4]

Whoever has not reached the maturity of perfection—that is, all of us ordinary Christians—could not preserve, without recourse to the medicine, the discipline, of fasting, that inner order by virtue of which the turbulence of sensuality is kept in check and the spirit liberated so that it may soar into the zone of its appropriate fulfillment and satisfaction. It is here, most particularly and strikingly, that the stern demands inherent in the Christian image of man become compellingly visible. Our natural duty obliges us to pay dearly so that we may become what we are by essence: the free moral person in full possession of himself.

Everyone knows that, on the whole, the Church's laws of fasting are not taken too seriously. It would be an error, however, to attribute this primarily to contempt for the ecclesiastical authority. The reason for this laxity lies elsewhere, namely, in the fact that nothing is as alien to the average Christian as the thought that there might be a natural, fundamental moral obligation to fast—before and apart from ecclesiastical injunctions. And many a priest would not be quite so ready to grant general mitigations of ecclesiastical rules of fasting were he to see in them not merely disciplinary regulations, but, with the "universal teacher," specific applications of a universal natural law.

Needless to say, this natural obligation to fast takes on a higher meaning and a deeper motivation from faith in Christ and from the supernatural love of God.[5] The theme of the perfection of nature through grace recurs here also. That perfection is represented in the very specifications which the "law of nature" experiences in the Church's rules of fasting.

The great fast of forty days, for instance, signifies that the Christian is preparing to share in the celebration of the mysteries of the death and resurrection of the Lord, wherein our redemption, which has its inception in the Incarnation, came finally to fruition. To obtain a share in these exalted realities demands in a special sense the prepared vessel of a free and "ordered" heart; on the other hand, no other reality, no other truth can so assuage and transform the innermost man.

"Can a man sin by fasting too strictly?" Nothing seems less pressing than this question, which heads one of the articles of St. Thomas.[6] But let it be noted in passing that he answers it affirmatively. For him, fasting is an act of *abstinentia*, an act of the virtue of abstinence, related, be it said, to the art of healing.[7] Again it is a question not of effort or castigation, but of the realization of the "order of reason."

With St. Jerome, St. Thomas says that to oppress one's body by exaggerated fasting and vigils is like bringing stolen goods as a sacrificial offering.[8] And in the *Summa Theologica*, we find the deeply Catholic thought that the Church, in her fasting regulations, is anxious also not to overtax nature, the natural will to live.[9] Characteristically, and not at all surprisingly, in the very article on fasting St. Thomas—who has been surnamed "Thomas of God the Creator"—mentions and refutes Manichaeism, his constant and primary adversary.[10] The following comments, also, should not be omitted here: "If one knowingly abstained from wine to the point of oppressing nature seriously, he would not be free of guilt;"[11] and: "For a man it is sinful to weaken his sexual potency by too strict fasting." [12]

Admittedly, these propositions take no prominent place in St. Thomas's works—they are slipped in more or less in passing. But one might be tempted to mistake his thesis on the natural obligation to fast for stark, unrelieved asceticism, were it not for these bright sparks of affirmation. Nonetheless, the validity of this thesis retains its full force.

Transgressions against the virtue of *abstinentia*, that is, against the "rational order" in the sphere of enjoyment of food and drink, are apt to be taken very lightly, if they are subjected to moral judgment at all. But to one who holds for a clear, decisive affirmation of the Christian image of man, the destructive effect of an obsessive preoccupation with the what and how much of food and drink is perfectly obvious. St. Thomas calls this effect *hebetudo sensus*[13]—the dulling and obscuring of the inner perception of spiritual realities. And might there not be a causal connection between this by now customary and fully accepted phenomenon of the dullness of inner perception, and the equally accepted and customary laxity? We might find cause for reflection in the wisdom of the Orient.

In Dante's cosmological poem, we find, in the second of the three cantos of the *Purgatorio* which treat of abstaining from the "gratification of the palate," an extremely striking, indeed a quite disconcerting, stanza. It says of the penitents: "The sockets of their eyes seemed rings without gems. Whoso in the face of men reads OMO, would surely there have recognized the M."[14] What is implied here is nothing less than this: through the penance of fasting, that which was devastated by the "gratification of the palate" is restored, namely, the inner form of man.

But to return once more to "cheerfulness of heart": Fasting should be performed with a cheerful heart. This is, as it were, a polemical exhortation. Christ Himself has named its counterpart "the disfigured faces of the hypocrites." And the experience of the ascetics furnishes another obverse.

All discipline, we have said, has reference to the operating person. This reference, however, bears in itself the constant danger of the loss of self-detachment, and of a change into self-righteousness, which draws from its ascetic "achievements" the profit of a solid self-admiration. Vanity, self-importance, impatient arrogance rising superior to the "imperfect"—these are the specific perils of the ascetic. Gregory the Great points this out clearly in his "Rule for Pastors," an inexhaustible treasure house of practical wisdom.[15]

Cheerfulness of heart, however, is the mark of selflessness. By this sign and seal one is sure to recognize that hypocrisy and all manner of tense self-involvement are done away with. Cheerfulness of heart is the infallible token that reveals the inner genuineness of discipline as *selfless* preservation of the self.

6. *The Sense of Touch*

ST. THOMAS says that *temperantia* has reference above all to the pleasure assigned to the sense of touch.[1] And to this sense are assigned both sexual pleasure and the pleasures of eating and drinking.[2]

We are too apt to take these statements with false literalness and to misinterpret them to the point of excessive triviality. Therefore it is necessary to point out briefly that they have a depth of bearing unsuspected at first glance, and why this is so.

The sense of touch, according to St. Thomas (and Aristotle) has a special rank among the senses. It is not a sense among other senses, but is the "basis of the other senses";[3] "all other senses are based on the sense of touch."[4] In this sense of touch there is contained principally the entire essence of the senses in general.[5] By the sense of touch, above all, a being becomes sentient—*animal*;[6] where there is no sense of touch, there is no sentient life.[7] This is the first point.

Second: "Among all sentient creatures man has the best sense of touch."[8] "There are animals which see more sharply or hear more acutely or smell more intensely than man. In the sense of touch, however, man differs from all other sentient beings by having a much more acute perception."[9]

And third: "Among men themselves those who possess the better sense of touch have the better power of cognition."[10] "One might suppose that cognitive talent should rather correspond to the excellence of the sense of sight than to that of touch, as the sense of sight is the intellectual sense and best perceives differences in things. . . . But one must say that cognitive talent corresponds more to the excellence of the sense of touch because the sense of touch is the basis of all other senses. Therefore he who has the better sense of touch has consequently simply a more sensitive nature and as a result a keener intelligence. For the excellence of sensitivity is the basis of excellence of intelligence. But from the fact that one has a better auditory or a better visual sense it does not follow that he is simply more sensitive; at most this is so only in a certain respect." [11]

These three thoughts, as surprising to come upon as a treasure trove, are here merely quoted and not commented on. For the purpose of this book, it is of no importance what modern sensorial physiology, for instance, would say to this. A look into the manuals will show that the basic approach in both the questions and the replies of St. Thomas is so immeasurably removed from today's notions that they cannot even be said to contradict each other.

But it is important to recognize that according to St. Thomas, the virtue of temperance, especially in its primordial forms of chastity and abstinence, relates to the root of the whole of sensual-intellectual life. Moderation extends its ordering mastery down to the fountainhead from which the figure of moral man springs up unceasingly.

Still another connection, hidden up to now, becomes visible in the conceptual field of relations pertaining to moderation.

The sense of touch is also the organ of pain.[12] And mastery of the spirit over pleasure linked with the sense of touch equally signifies mastery over pain.

Discipline, says Ernst Jünger in his notable essay "Concerning Pain," has no other significance than this: to keep life in constant contact with pain and by this means in readiness "to be sacrificed for the purpose of a higher order." [13]

Needless to say, the masklike rigidity of Jünger's concept of "discipline" is essentially different from the Christian concept of temperance and moderation. Jünger would never have been able to endorse St. Thomas's proposition: "The goal and norm of temperance is blessedness."[14] And yet, if we regard the Christian notion of temperance from the angle of pain, a sterner face rises behind the foreground of creational joy, a face molded by the decision to relinquish the created for the sake of the Creator. But this sterner face, also, radiates an assenting joy, immeasurably above all ingenuous rejoicing in the created.

7. Humility

ONE OF THE GOODS in which man naturally seeks fulfillment of his being is *excellentia*: superiority, pre-eminence, consideration.[1] The virtue of temperance, insofar as it relates this natural urge to the order of reason, is called humility. The ground of humility is man's estimation of himself according to truth.[2] And that is almost all there is to it.

Starting from this definition, it is difficult to understand how "humility" could have become, as it were, a bone of contention. To disregard the demonic resistance against good which makes this feature of the Christian image of man its particular target, is possible only because the notion of humility has become blurred even in the Christian consciousness. In the whole tractate of St. Thomas concerning humility and pride, there is not a single sentence to suggest an attitude, on principle, of constant self-accusation, of disparagement of one's being and doing, of cringing inferiority feelings, as belonging to humility or any other Christian virtue.

Nothing lights the way to a proper understanding of humility more tellingly than this: humility and high-mindedness not only are not mutually exclusive,[3] but actually are neighbors and akin; and both are equally opposed to either pride or pusillanimity.[4]

What is meant by high-mindedness or magnanimity? It is the striving of the mind toward great things.[5] High-minded is the man who feels the potentiality of greatness and prepares for it. The high-minded or magnanimous man is, in a certain sense, "selective." He will not be accessible to every approach, but will keep himself for the greatness to which he feels akin.[6] Above all, high-mindedness is demanding as to honor: "The high-minded man strives toward that which deserves the highest honor."[7] In the *Summa Theologica* we read: "If a man should despise honor to the extent that he would not take care to do what is deserving of honor, this would be blameworthy."[8] On the other hand, the high-minded man is not crushed by dishonor; he disregards it as something beneath him.[9] The high-minded man despises everything small-minded. He would never prize another man so highly as to do anything improper for his sake.[10] The words of the Psalmist (Psalm 14, 4), "The evil-doer is nothing in his sight," refer to the high-minded "contempt of men" of the just, says St. Thomas.[11] Fearless frankness is the hallmark of high-mindedness; nothing is further from it than to suppress truth from fear.[12] Flattery and dissimulation are equally removed from the high-minded.[13] The high-minded man does not complain; for his heart is impervious to external evil.[14] High-mindedness implies an unshakable firmness of hope, an actually challenging assurance,[15] and the perfect peace of a fearless heart.[16] The high-minded man bows neither to confusion of the soul, nor to any man, nor to fate—but to God alone.[17]

One marvels to learn that this description of high-mindedness is drawn, trait by trait, in the *Summa Theologica* of Aquinas. This needed to be made clear. For in the treatise on humility it is said repeatedly that humility is not opposed to high-mindedness. Now we can fathom the true significance of this statement, spoken as if it were a warning and a caution. This is its meaning: a "humility" too weak and too narrow to be able to bear the inner tension of cohabitation with high-mindedness is not true humility.

The customary judgment of men is always prone to call a high-minded man a haughty man, and so equally to miss the true nature of humility. "A haughty man"—this is easily and quickly said. But only rarely is the quality here implied that of pride (*superbia*). Pride is not, in the first place, a quality of everyday behavior in human relationships. Pride refers to man's relationship to God. Pride is the anti-realistic denial of the relationship between creature and Creator; pride denies the creaturely nature of man. Every sin contains two elements: a turning away from God and a turning toward transitory good; the decisive and defining element is the first one: the turning away from God. And this is more pronounced in pride than in any other sin. "All sins flee before God; pride alone stands up against God."[18] Holy Scripture says of the proud alone that "God flouts the scornful" (James 4, 6).

Humility, too, is not primarily an attitude in human relationships. Humility, too, looks first to God. That which pride denies and destroys, humility affirms and preserves: the creaturely quality of man. If to be a creature—to be created—is the innermost nature of man, then humility, as "subjection of man to God,"[19] is the affirmation of this essential and primordial fact. Second: Humility, consequently, is not outward behavior but an inner attitude, born of decision of the will.[20] Regarding God and its own creaturely quality, it is an attitude of perfect recognition of that which, by reason of God's will, really *is*; above all, it is candid acceptance of this one thing: that man and humanity are neither God nor "like God." At this point we get a glimpse of the hidden connection that links the Christian virtue of humility with the—perhaps equally Christian—gift of humor.

Third, and finally: Can we avoid stating outright that beyond everything said so far, humility is also an attitude of man to man, namely, the attitude of self-abasement of one before the other? Let us examine this more closely.

In the *Summa Theologica*, St. Thomas specifically raises the question of the humble attitude of man to man, and answers it as follows: "In man, two things have to be considered: that which is of God, and that which is of man. . . . But humility in the strict sense means the awe in virtue of which man subjects himself to God. Consequently man, with regard to that which is of himself, must subject himself to his neighbor with regard to that which is of God in him. But humility does not require that one subject that which is of God in himself to that which seems to be of God in the other. . . . Humility likewise does not require that one subject that which is of himself to that which is of man in the other." [21]

In the broad and many-graded area of this reply there is room for the "contempt of men" on the part of the highminded just as there is for the self-abasement of St. Francis of Assisi, who took off his cowl and had himself brought before the people with a rope around his neck.[22] Here again it becomes evident that Christian teaching is wary of the tightness and confinement of one-track rules. This caution or, better, aversion is voiced by St. Augustine in another though related reference: "If one man says you should not receive the Eucharist every day, and another says the opposite, let each one do what he thinks he should, in piety, according to his own belief. For neither did Zacchæus and the Roman officer dispute with one another, although the one received the Lord with joy into his house and the other said: 'I am not worthy that thou shouldst enter under my roof' (Luke 19, 6; 7, 6). Both honored the Redeemer, though not in the same manner." [23]

8. The Power of Wrath

IN CHRISTIAN PARLANCE, the notions of "sensuality," "passion," "desire" are customarily—though very unjustly—understood exclusively as "anti-spiritual sensuality," "wicked passion," "rebellious desire." Such a constriction of an originally much broader meaning obscures the important fact that all these notions by no means have a merely negative sense; rather, they represent forces from which the essence of human nature is built up and draws its life. The same is true of the notion of wrath or anger. At the mention of anger, Christian awareness sees as a rule only the uncontrolled, the anti-spiritual, the negative aspect. But, as with "sensuality" and "desire," the power of wrath also belongs to the primal forces of human nature. In this power of wrath, the energy of human nature is most clearly expressed. It is a force directed toward the difficult of achievement, toward the thing beyond the easy grasp, ever ready to expose itself wherever an "arduous good" waits to be conquered. "The power of anger is given to sentient beings so that the hindrances may be removed whereby the force of desire is impeded from striving toward its object, whether because of the difficulty of achieving a good or because of the difficulty of overcoming an evil."[1] Wrath is the strength to attack the repugnant;[2] the power of anger is actually the power of resistance in the soul.[3]

Whoever, therefore, stigmatizes the power of wrath as something in itself anti-spiritual and consequently to be "mortified" is committing the same error as one who similarly slights "sensuality," "passion," and "desire." Both contemn the basic forces of our being; both are offending the Creator, who, as the liturgy of the Church says, has "marvelously established the dignity of human nature."

Concerning wrath (in the narrower sense), understood as the passionate desire for just retribution of injustice that has been suffered, St. Thomas, in repudiation of the Stoics, says the following: "Because the nature of man is constructed of soul and body, of spirit and sensuality, it belongs to the good of man to devote himself *utterly* to virtue, namely with spirit, sensuality, and body alike. And therefore man's virtue requires that the will for just retribution reside not only in the spiritual realm of the soul, but also in sensuality and in the body itself." This passage is found in the great work of St. Thomas's later life, the *De Malo,* in an article discussing the question "whether all wrath is evil."[4] Anger is "good" if, in accordance with the order of reason, it is brought into service for the true goals of man;[5] one who does good with passion is more praiseworthy than one who is "not entirely" afire for the good, even to the forces of the sensual realm.[6] Gregory the Great says: "Reason opposes evil the more effectively when anger ministers at her side."[7] And what was said of the power of sexual desire, which overwhelms reason, is likewise true of the obscuring power of anger: "It is not contrary to the nature of virtue that the consideration of reason comes to a stop in the execution of that which reason has already considered; even art would be impeded in its activity if it should wish to consider what was to be done where it was a question of immediate action."[8]

The surprise with which we reflect on these statements makes us aware once again how far we are from considering the whole man in our conception of the moral good. We realize how much we almost unconsciously tend to take the "purely spiritual" for actual humanity; how much, on the other hand, the "ancients" can teach us and make us once again embrace the full created nature of world and man, in its true reality.

It is self-evident that the anger which breaks all bounds and disrupts the order of reason is evil and is sin. Blind wrath, bitterness of spirit, and revengeful resentment, the three basic forms of intemperate anger,[9] are therefore evil and contrary to order.

Blind wrath shuts the eyes of the spirit before they have been able to grasp the facts and to judge them; bitterness and resentment, with a grim joy[10] in negation, close their ears to the language of truth and love; they poison the heart like a festering ulcer.[11] Also evil, of course, is all anger linked to unjust desire. This needs no further discussion.

In the upsurge of his self-will, the intemperately angry man feels as if he were drawing his whole being together like a club ready to strike. But this is the very thing he fails to achieve. Only gentleness and mildness can accomplish it. (The two are not equivalent; mildness is gentleness turned toward what is without.)[12] "Gentleness above all makes man master of himself."[13] Holy Scripture speaks of this virtue in much the same terms as of patience. In St. Luke's Gospel, it is said of patience that through it man possesses his soul; and of gentleness it is said: "Possess thy soul through gentleness" (Eccles. 10, 31).

Gentleness, however, does not signify that the original power of wrath is weakened or, worse still, "mortified," just as chastity does not imply a weakening of sexual power. On the contrary: gentleness as a virtue presupposes the power of wrath; gentleness implies mastery of this power, not its weakening. We should not mistake the pale-faced harmlessness which pretends to be gentleness—unfortunately often successfully—for a Christian virtue. Lack of sensuality is not chastity; and incapacity for wrath has nothing to do with gentleness. Such incapacity not only is not a virtue, but, as St. Thomas expressly says, a fault: *peccatum* and *vitium*.[14]

In the *Summa Theologica*, St. Thomas raises and answers a remarkable question: Which is the greater evil and wrong: intemperateness in wrath, or intemperateness in pleasure?[15] His reply is: If we consider the fruits of each, it is intemperate wrath that is, as a rule, the greater evil, as it commonly works against the welfare of one's neighbor. But if we consider the passion itself, which in both cases degenerates into intemperateness, then intemperate pleasure is the greater wrong, for various reasons. The excitement of anger, for example, since it is aroused by an injustice, still in some way appertains to reason; whereas pleasure refers exclusively to sensuality. Speaking absolutely, the sin of intemperate wrath is less evil than intemperate pleasure, in the same proportion as the good of justice toward which the angry man is directed ranks above the pleasure-seeking of the lustful man. This, also, is the reason why the intemperately lustful man is more contemptible than the immoderately angry one.[16] Further, immoderate wrath is as a rule conditioned by the physical constitution—that is, by natural disposition—more than immoderate pleasure-seeking. (For this reason, the inclination to immoderate anger is more easily and frequently hereditary than that of immoderate pleasure-seeking.) And finally, the intemperately wrathful man is less obnoxious than the intemperately lustful one, because the former, akin to the high-minded, is all frankness, while the immoderate pleasure-seeker, intent on dissimulation and camouflage, is unable to give or take a straight look in the eye.

It is particularly in reference to overcoming intemperateness of sensual desire that the power of wrath acquires a special importance.

Aquinas, it is true, also says that an acute temptation to unchastity is most easily conquerable by flight.[17] But he likewise knows that the addiction to degenerate pleasure-seeking can by no means be cured through a merely negative approach, through convulsively "shutting one's mind" to it. Thomas believes that the deterioration of one power of the soul should be healed and supplemented by the still undamaged core of some other power. Thus it should be possible to subdue and, as it were, to quench the limp intemperateness of an unchaste lustfulness by attacking a difficult task with the resilient joy generated in the full power of wrath. [18]

Only the combination of the intemperateness of lustfulness with the lazy inertia incapable of generating anger is the sign of complete and virtually hopeless degeneration. It appears whenever a caste, a people, or a whole civilization is ripe for its decline and fall.

9. Disciplining the Eyes

THAT THE WORDS *studiositas* and *curiositas* were not translated at their first mention was not unintentional nor indeed without necessity. Of course it would be easy enough to render them, following the dictionary, as "desire for knowledge" or "zeal," for the first, and "inquisitiveness," for the second. But this would amount to suppressing their most important meaning. Further, one might think that we speak but trivially and condescendingly of the virtue of the "good student" and of the more or less harmless weakness of the woman gossiping across the back fence.

Studiositas, curiositas—by these are meant temperateness and intemperance, respectively, in the natural striving for knowledge; temperateness and intemperance, above all, in the indulgence of the sensual perception of the manifold sensuous beauty of the world; temperateness and intemperance in the "desire for knowledge and experience," as St. Augustine puts it. [1]

Nietzsche said that wisdom "puts limits to knowledge." Whatever he himself may have meant by this, there is no doubt that the will-to-knowledge, this noble power of the human being, requires a restraining wisdom, "in order that man may not strive immoderately for the knowledge of things." [2]

But in what consists such immoderateness? Certainly not (as has been said by St. Thomas, in refutation of the scorners of

natural creation, and as we must repeat today, addressing ourselves to the same tendencies) in the fact that the mind of man
strives to unseal the natural secrets and locked places of creation: consequently not in "secular science" *per se*. Concerning
the study of philosophy, for instance, we read in the *Summa
Theologica* that it is "to be praised for the truth which was
recognized by the (pagan) philosophers, namely, as the Epistle to the Romans says (1, 19) because God revealed it to
them." [3]

All the same, in view of the armed attack upon the natural
mysteries of creation, it would be well to keep in mind the
startling phrase of the aged Goethe: "We would have a better
knowledge of things if we did not try to know them so thoroughly." [4]

Immoderateness in striving for knowledge, says St. Thomas,
is exemplified in magic.[5] Nowadays, this thought makes us
smile. But are we really so far removed from being willing to
pay the price even of our salvation for the unlocking of im-
penetrabilities, should the choice be open to us—that is the
question. Further, it is also immoderate and senseless to try to
master God Himself and His work by deciphering His inten-
tions. We may, for instance, be able to grasp in faith the actuality and the ultimate meaning of God's working in history. But
no man can presume on his own to point to any providential
happening of the here and now, and to say: "God has manifested His intention in this or that reward or punishment,
confirmation or rejection." This temptation to unveil God's
inscrutability for tangible everyday use, thereby negating it, is
concealed under a thousand disguises and is equally close and
perilous for the most profound as for the most superficial
minds. St. Augustine writes in his *Confessions*: "Indeed, I no
longer trouble myself about the course of the stars, and my
soul hath never sought an answer from the shades; I condemn
all this blasphemous magic. But how hath the Enemy seduced
me with his thousandfold wiles that I, O Lord my God, should

require a sign from Thee, whom I should serve all loyally and simply!" [6]

The essential intemperateness of the urge for knowledge, however, is "concupiscence of the eyes." Only by working through a tangled thicket of vague and false interpretation, and by following the guidance of St. Augustine and St. Thomas, can we obtain a grasp of the true significance of this word of Scripture. It has, as will be seen, an immediate relevance to modern man.

There is a gratification in seeing that reverses the original meaning of vision and works disorder in man himself. The true meaning of seeing is perception of reality. But "concupiscence of the eyes" does not aim to perceive reality, but to enjoy "seeing." St. Augustine says of the "concupiscence of the palate" that it is not a question of satiating one's hunger but of tasting and relishing food; [7] this is also true of *curiositas* and the "concupiscence of the eyes." "What this seeing strives for is not to attain knowledge and to become cognizant of the truth, but for possibilities of relinquishing oneself to the world," says Heidegger in his book *Being and Time*. [8]

Aquinas assigns *curiositas* to the "roaming unrest of spirit," *evagatio mentis*, which he says is the first-born daughter of *acedia*. Since these interrelations are anything but constructions of a game of allegories, it is well worth while to give them a moment's closer scrutiny. *Acedia* is the dreary sadness of a heart unwilling to accept the greatness to which man is called by God; this inertia raises its paralyzing face wherever man is trying to shake off the obligatory nobility of being that belongs to his essential dignity as a person, and particularly the nobility of the sonship of God, thus denying his true self. [9] *Acedia*, says Thomas, first shows its effect in the "roaming unrest of the spirit." [10] (Its second daughter is despair, and this kinship throws revealing sidelights on the subject of our present discussion.) "Roaming unrest of the spirit," on the other hand, manifests itself in verbosity, in unbridled desire "to burst forth from the citadel of the spirit into diversity"; in inner restlessness, in instability of place as well as instability of resolution, and especially in the insatiability of *curiositas*.[11]

Accordingly, the degeneration into *curiositas* of the natural wish to see may be much more than a harmless confusion on the surface of the human being. It may be the sign of complete rootlessness. It may mean that man has lost his capacity for living with himself; that, in flight from himself, nauseated and bored by the void of an interior life gutted by despair, he is seeking with selfish anxiety and on a thousand futile paths that which is given only to the noble stillness of a heart held ready for sacrifice and thus in possession of itself, namely, the fullness of being. Because he is not really living from the wellspring of his nature, he seeks, as Heidegger says, in "curiosity, to which nothing remains closed," the pledge of a supposedly genuine "living Life." [12]

Not for nothing does Holy Scripture name "concupiscence of the eyes" among the three powers which constitute the world that "lieth in the power of evil" (I John 2, 16; 5, 19).

It reaches the extremes of its destructive and eradicating power when it builds itself a world according to its own image and likeness: when it surrounds itself with the restlessness of a perpetual moving picture of meaningless shows, and with the literally deafening noise of impressions and sensations breathlessly rushing past the windows of the senses. Behind the flimsy pomp of its façade dwells absolute nothingness; it is a world of, at most, ephemeral creations, which often within less than a quarter hour become stale and discarded, like a newspaper or magazine swiftly scanned or merely perused; a world which, to the piercing eye of the healthy mind untouched by its contagion, appears like the amusement quarter of a big city in the hard brightness of a winter morning: desperately bare, disconsolate, and ghostly.

The destructiveness of this disorder which originates from, and grows upon, obsessive addiction, lies in the fact that it stifles man's primitive power of perceiving reality; that it makes man incapable not only of coming to himself but also of reaching reality and truth.

If such an illusory world threatens to overgrow and smother the world of real things, then to restrain the natural wish to see takes on the character of a measure of self-protection and self-defense. *Studiositas*, in this frame of reference, primarily signifies that man should oppose this virtually inescapable seduction with all the force of selfless self-preservation; that he should hermetically close the inner room of his being against the intrusively boisterous pseudo-reality of empty shows and sounds. It is in such an asceticism of cognition alone that he may preserve or regain that which actually constitutes man's vital existence: the perception of the reality of God and His creation, and the possibility of shaping himself and the world according to this truth, which reveals itself only in silence.

10. The Fruits of Temperance

TO THE VIRTUE OF TEMPERANCE as the preserving and defending realization of man's inner order, the gift of beauty is particularly co-ordinated. Not only is temperance beautiful in itself, it also renders men beautiful.[1] Beauty, however, must here be understood in its original meaning: as the glow of the true and the good irradiating from every ordered state of being, and not in the patent significance of immediate sensual appeal. The beauty of temperance has a more spiritual, more austere, more virile aspect. It is of the essence of this beauty that it does not conflict with true virility, but rather has an affinity to it. Temperance, as the wellspring and premise of fortitude,[2] is the virtue of mature manliness.

The infantile[3] disorder of intemperance, on the other hand, not only destroys beauty,[4] it also makes man cowardly; intemperance more than any other thing renders man unable and unwilling to "take heart" against the wounding power of evil in the world. [5]

It is not easy to read in a man's face whether he is just or unjust. Temperance or intemperance, however, loudly proclaim themselves in everything that manifests a personality: in the order or disorder of the features, in the attitude, the laugh, the handwriting. Temperance, as the inner order of man, can as little remain "purely interior" as the soul itself, and as all other life of the soul or mind. It is the nature of the soul to be the "form of the body."

This fundamental principle of all Christian psychology[6] not only states the in-forming of the body by the soul, but also the reference of the soul to the body. On this, a second factor is based: temperance or intemperance of outward behavior and expression can have its strengthening or weakening repercussion on the inner order of man.[7] It is from this point of view that all outer discipline—whether in the sphere of sexual pleasure or in that of eating and drinking, of self-assertion, of anger, and of the gratification of the eye—obtains its meaning, its justification, and its necessity.

It is a noteworthy fact—but who has ever called attention to it?—that almost all pathological obsessions, witnesses as they are to a disturbed inner order, belong to the sphere of *temperantia*: sexual aberrations as well as dipsomania, delusion of grandeur, pathological irascibility, and the passive craving of the rootless for sensations. All these petrifactions of selfishness are accompanied by the despair of missing the goal striven for with such violent exertion of will—namely, the gratification of the self. In the nature of things, all selfish self-seeking is a desperate effort. For it is a natural, primal fact, prior to all human decision, that man loves God more than himself, and consequently that he must of necessity miss his very goal— himself—by following the ungodly, the "anti-godly," path of selfishness.

Intemperantia and despair are connected by a hidden channel. Whoever in stubborn recklessness persists in pursuing perfect satisfaction and gratification in prestige and pleasure has set his foot on the road to despair. Another thing, also, is true: one who rejects fulfillment in its true and final meaning, and, despairing of God and himself, anticipates nonfulfillment,[8] may well regard the artificial paradise of unrestrained pleasure-seeking as the sole place, if not of happiness, then of forgetfulness, of self-oblivion: "In their despair, they gave themselves up to incontinence" (Ephesians 4, 19).[9] That sin is a burden and a bondage is nowhere more apparent than in *intemperantia*, in that obsession of selfish self-preservation, which seeks itself in vain.

Temperance, on the contrary, is liberating and purifying. This above all: temperance effects purification.

If one approaches the difficult concept of purity through this strangely neglected gateway and begins to understand purity as the fruit of purification, the confusing and discordant sounds which usually obscure this notion and move it dangerously close to Manichaeism are silenced. From this approach the full and unrestricted concept of purity—so different from the currently accepted one—comes into view.

This is the purity meant by John Cassian when he calls purity of heart the immanent purpose of temperance: "It is served by solitude, fasting, night watches, and penitence."[10] It is this wider concept of purity which is referred to in St. Augustine's statement that the virtue of temperance and moderation aims at preserving man uninjured and undefiled for God.[11]

But what does this unrestricted concept of purity stand for? It stands for that crystal-clear, morning-fresh freedom from self-consciousness, for that selfless acceptance of the world which man experiences when the shock of a profound sorrow carries him to the brink of existence or when he is touched by the shadow of death. It is said in the Scriptures: "Grave illness sobers the soul" (Eccles. 31, 2); this sobriety belongs to the essence of purity. That most disputed statement of Aristotle: tragedy causes purification, catharsis,[12] points in the same direction. Even the Holy Spirit's gift of fear, which St. Thomas assigns to *temperantia*,[13] purifies the soul by causing it to experience, through grace, the innermost peril of man. Its fruit is that purity by dint of which the selfish and furtive search for spurious fulfillment is abandoned. Purity is the perfect unfolding of the whole nature from which alone could have come the words: "Behold the handmaid of the Lord!" (Luke 1, 38).

A new depth here opens to our view: purity is not only the

fruit of purification; it implies at the same time readiness to accept God's purifying intervention, terrible and fatal though it might be; to accept it with the bold candor of a trustful heart, and thus to experience its fruitful and transforming power.

This, then, is the ultimate meaning of the virtue of temperance.

Notes

The quotations from the *Summa Theologica* of St. Thomas Aquinas [quotations from the Aquinas translation are taken from the edition published by Burns, Oates & Washbourne Ltd., to whom grateful acknowledgment is made] are indicated in the following notes only by numerals. (For example, "II, II, 47, 5 ad 3" means: Second Part of the Second Part, quaestio 47, articulus 5, reply to Objection 3.) The same code is used for references to the commentary on the *Sentences* of Peter Lombard (for example, "3, d. 33, 2, 5" means: Book Three, distinctio 33, quaestio 2, articulus 5). The titles of the other works of St. Thomas cited in the text are abbreviated as follows:

Quaestiones disputatae de veritate (Ver.)
Quaestio disputata de virtutibus in communi (Virt. comm.)
Quaestio disputata de virtutibus cardinalibus (Virt. card.)
Quaestio disputata de anima (An.)
Quaestiones quodlibetales (Quol.)
Summa contra Gentes (C.G.)
De regimine principum (Reg. princ.)
Commentary on the Nichomachean Ethics of Aristotle (In Eth.)
Commentary on the Politics of Aristotle (In Pol.)
Commentary on Dionysius the Aeropagite, On the Divine Names (In Div. Nom.)
Commentary on the Gospel of Matthew (In Matth.)
Commentary on the Epistle to the Ephesians (In Ephes.)
Commentary on Aristotle's "On the Soul" (In An.)
Commentary on the Second Epistle to the Corinthians (In II Cor.)

207

Commentary on the Epistles to the Romans (In Rom.)
Expositio in Evangelium B. Joannis (In John)
Quaestiones disputatae de malo (Mal.)

PRUDENCE

1. THE FIRST OF THE CARDINAL VIRTUES

1 *Prudentia dicitur genitrix virtutum.* 3, d. 33, 2, 5.

2 Cf. II, II, 47, 5 ad 3.

3 II, II, 50, 1 ad 1.

4 *Virt. comm.* 12 ad 23.

5 "Du Caractère métaphysique de la théologie morale de Saint Thomas." *Revue thomiste,* Vol. 8 (1925), p. 345.

6 Cf. for example Merkelbach, *Summa Theologiae Moralis* (Paris, 1930ff.), vol. I, p. 7. It is strange to see that the Spaniard Francisco de Vitoria, who, in the second quarter of the sixteenth century, revived the study of St. Thomas, allows disproportionately little space in his great commentary on the *Secunda secundae* of the *Summa Theologica* for discusison of prudence; and that a hundred years later his fellow countryman Johannes a Sancto Thoma, one of the foremost exegetes of Thomas, in his famous *Cursus theologicus* does not even bother to treat expressly the virtue of prudence. Concerning contemporary moral theology, Garrigou-Lagrange says, *"Il est véritablement étonnant . . . que la principale des vertus cardinales tienne si peu de place dans la science morale d'aujourd'hui."* "Du caractère métaphysique de la théologie morale de Saint Thomas." *Revue thomiste,* vol. 8 (1925), p. 345.

7 *Virt. comm.* 6; II, II, 51, 2; *Ver.* 14, 6. Ambrose in his book on the duties actually says that justice is useless if a man be without prudence (*De officiis* I, 27). He justifies this statement by a sentence in Scripture (Prov. 17, 16?) which, however, may have been contained only in an ancient translation. In the same chapter of *De officiis* we find the sentence: *"Primus igitur officii fons prudentia est"*–The prime fount of duty is prudence.

8 II, II, 4, 5; *Ver.* 14, 6; *Quol.* 12, 22.

9 *"Prudentia est completiva omnium virtutum moralium."* II, II, 166, 2 ad 1. *"Ab ipsa (prudentia) est . . . complementum bonitatis in omnibus aliis virtutibus."* *Virt. comm.* 6.

10 I, II, 64, 3; *Virt. comm.* 13.

11 Concerning the concept of measure as "permanently exterior prototype," cf. Josef Pieper, *Die Wirklichkeit und das Gute* (6th edition, Munich, 1956), pp. 23 f.

12 *Ver.* 14, 5 ad 11; 3, d. 27, 2, 4, 3; cf. 3, d. 27, 2, 4, 3 ad 2.

13 *Virt. comm.* 9.

14 II, II, 47, 5 ad 2.

15 II, II, 47, 5 ad 1.

16 II, II, 56, 2 ad 3.

17 II, II, 55, 2 ad 3.

18 II, II, 119, 3 ad 3; II, II, 141, 1 ad 2.

19 *"Bonum hominis, inquantum est homo, est: ut ratio sit perfecta in cognitione veritatis, et inferiores appetitus regulentur secundum regulam rationis; nam homo habet quod sit homo per hoc quod sit rationalis."* *Virt. comm.* 9.

20 *Oratio* for the third Sunday after Easter.

21 Goethe to Müller on March 28, 1819.

22 I, II, 64, 3 ad 2; cf. *Die Wirklichkeit und das Gute,* pp. 91 f.

2. KNOWLEDGE OF REALITY AND THE REALIZATION OF THE GOOD

1 *Virt. comm.* 6.

2 II, II, 47, 3.

3 Cf. again *Die Wirklichkeit und das Gute,* pp. 11 ff.

4 I, II, 63, 3.

5 I, II, 14, 2; II, II, 47, 6 ad 1.

6 II, II, 47, 6 ad 3.

7 II, II, 47, 6 ad 3; *Ver.* 5, 1 ad 6.

8 *"La conscience droite et certaine n'est autre qu'un acte de la prudence, qui conseille, qui juge pratiquement et qui commande."* Garrigou-Lagrange, "Du Caractère métaphysique de la théologie morale de Saint Thomas." *Revue thomiste,* vol. 8 (1925), p. 354. Cf. also Merkelbach, *Summa Theologiae Moralis,* vol. II, p. 42.

9 *Virt. card.* 1.

10 *Die Wirklichkeit und das Gute,* pp. 5a ff.

11 II, II. 48.

12 It is perhaps a sign of the importance that the High Middle Ages attributed to the cognitive basis of prudent decisions that Thomas has a special name for lack of deliberation and for lack

of judgment (*praecipitatio* and *inconsideratio*), whereas we tend not to distinguish between these two ideas.

13 Aristotle, *Nicomachean Ethics*, VI, 9.

14 II, II, 47, 9.

15 II, II, 49, 4.

16 II, II, 53, 5.

17 II, II, 47, 1 ad 3; II, II, 47, 8.

18 II, II, 47, 3 ad 3; II, II, 47, 14 ad 3.

19 II, II, 47, 14 ad 1.

20 II, II, 47, 14 ad 2.

21 *De trinitate*, XI, 3-5; XV, 22.

22 II, II, 49, 1.

23 II, II, 49, 3 ad 3; cf. II, II, 49, 3.

24 In the *Summa Theologica* (II, II, 49, 1 ad 1) Thomas writes: *"Multa quae pertinent ad partem sensitivam, requiruntur ad pruden-tiam"*—Many things belonging to the realm of the senses are requisite for prudence. It is true that the context of this sentence refers imme-diately to memory, which in Aristotle's view (*De Memoria* 1) is closely linked to the perceptions of the senses. But it is quite possible and cogent to extend this sentence, which is formulated in exceedingly general terms, to the sphere of natural life as a whole.

25 II, II, 55, 1.

26 It is significant that for modern characterology "flexibility" and "objectivity," and their opposites, are regarded as correspondent and mutually conditioning qualities—not only in the sense of "logi-cal" kinship, but in real reference to the practical framework of actions taken by the moral person.

27 II, II, 49, 6.

28 II, II, 47, 9 ad 2.

29 The "uncertainty" in the precepts of prudence consists in the possibility of the prudent man's mistaking what is objectively good and right. He cannot mistake what is *subjectively* good; for the actions commanded by prudence are always subjectively and neces-sarily good. At issue here is an insoluble problem, a problem most revealing of the finiteness and inadequacy of human existence. It is the problem of the subjectively certain but erroneous conscience. Within the sphere of this existential problem even language tends to lose its unambiguity. "Prudent," "good," "obligatory"—all these terms appear overcast by the twilight of ambiguity. The concrete

situation of the concrete act can always contain an element that escapes even the most alert and careful intelligence: and every concrete act can have immediate and inexorable consequences which could not have been calculated in advance. (Cf. the commentary of H. D. Noble, O.P., on the *quaestiones* concerning prudence in the French edition of the *Summa Theologica* [Paris, 1925, pp. 241 f.].) This uncertainty as to agreement with reality, and consequently of what ought practically to be accomplished, is the distressing thorn that accompanies all human prudence; it nullifies the self-assurance of moralism, makes any such assurance inwardly impossible. On the other hand, when the vital foundation of the moral life has been weakened, this uncertainty can lead to overscrupulousness.

30 II, II, 49, 6 ad 1.

31 II, II, 53, 6.

32 "Duality of the mind [*duplicitas animi*] is also something resulting from unchastity" (II, II, 53, 6 ad 2).

33 II, II, 55.

34 II, II, 55, 1.

35 II, II, 55, 3–5.

36 II, II, 55, 3 ad 2.

37 II, II, 55, 8 ad 2.

38 *Nicomachean Ethics*, IV, 3.

39 II, II, 55, 8.

40 II, II, 118, 2.

41 II, II, 118, 1 ad 3.

42 II, II, 55, 8.

43 The connection between the objectivity of knowledge, which as we have seen is the foundation of prudence, and justice, which is the virtue of community living, appears most plainly in the dual function of language, which is on the one hand communication, and on the other hand an image of man's knowledge of reality and hence of reality itself. To the extent that it is a "sign" (but it is more than a sign), language is, like all other signs, a "sign of something to someone." Language, however, or rather speech, which is not an "image of an object" ceases to be real communication to the extent that it is not. Where speech is no longer really a sign "of something," that is to say, a sign of reality, it is also no longer a sign "to someone." Cf. Josef Pieper, "Sachlichkeit und Klugheit." *Der katholische Gedanke*, vol. 5 (1932, pp. 72 f.). We must mention here the remarkable fact

that characterology of the school of "individual psychology" directly relates, in fact virtually equates, its rather vague basic concept of "community feeling" with "objectivity." (Cf., for example, Erwin Wexberg, *Individualpsychologie*, Leipzig, 1928, pp. 77 ff.)

44 Paul Claudel, *Cinq grandes odes*. In the fifth ode ("La Maison fermée"), in the section on the four cardinal virtues, there is the verse: *"La prudence est au Nord de mon âme comme la proue intelligente, qui conduit tout le bâteau."*

45 "Contemplative happiness is nothing else than perfect contemplation of the highest truth; but active happiness is the act of prudence by which man governs himself and others" (*Virt. comm.* 5 ad 8; *Ver.* 14, 2). We may also note here that Thomas regards prudence (alongside of justice) as the most proper virtue of rulers (II, II, 50, 1 ad 1), and the art of ruling (*prudentia regnativa*) as the highest form of prudence (II, II, 50, 2 ad 1).

46 "Who looks at himself does not shine." Lao-tse, *Tao Tê Ching*, chapter 24.

3. DELIMITATIONS AND CONTRASTS

1 *Virt. card.* 1.

2 *Ver.* 21, 3.

3 *"Verum est manifestativum et declarativum esse."* Hilary. Cited in *Ver.* 1.

4 I, II, 17, 5 ad 3.

5 *Metaphysics*, II, 1.

6 *Virt. comm.* 6 ad 5; II, II, 109, 2 ad 1.

7 *An.* 13 ad 11.

8 I, II, 18, 5.

9 II, II, 4, 5.

10 *"Quia ex hac rectitudine et bonitatis complemento omnes habitus appetitivi virtutis rationem sortiuntur, inde est quod prudentia est causa omnium virtutum appetitivae partis, quae dicuntur morales, inquantum sunt virtutes. Et propterea dicit Gregorius (Moral. 22, 1), quod ceterae virtutes, nisi ea quae appetunt, prudenter agant, virtutes esse nequaquam possunt."* Virt. comm. 6; cf. Quol. 12, 22.

11 3, d. 33, 2, 5.

12 *"Regula intellectualis virtutis (qua determinatur medium*

virtutis moralis; I, II, 64, 3, obj. 2) . . . est . . . ipsa res." I, II, 64, 3 ad 2.

13 II, II, 49, 3.

14 *"Homo autem est multarum operationum et diversarum; et hoc propter nobilitatem sui principii activi, scil. animae, cuius virtus ad infinita quodammodo se extendit."* Virt. comm. 6.

15 *"Cum hoc (bonum proprium hominis) multipliciter varietur et in multis bonum hominis consistat, non potuit homini inesse naturalis appetitus huius boni determinati, secundum condiciones omnes quae requiruntur ad hoc quod sit ei bonum, cum hoc multipliciter varietur secundum diversas condiciones personarum et temporum et locorum et huiusmodi. . . . Ita oportet quod ratio practica perficiatur aliquo habitu ad hoc quod recte diiudicet de bono humano secundum singula agenda. Et haec virtus dicitur prudentia."* Virt. comm. 6.

16 *"Unumquodque autem horum contingit multipliciter fieri et non eodem modo in omnibus; unde ad hoc quod rectus modus statuatur, requiritur iudicii prudentia."* Virt. comm. 6.

17 *"Ea quae sunt ad finem in rebus humanis non sunt determinata, sed multipliciter diversificantur secundum diversitatem personarum et negotiorum."* II, II, 47, 15; cf. *Virt. comm.* 13 ad 17; II, II, 47, 2 ad 3.

18 "Every mean of moral virtue is a rational mean, since moral virtue is said to observe the mean, through conformity with right reason. But it happens sometimes that the rational mean is also the real mean; in which case the mean of moral virtue is the real mean, for instance, in justice. On the other hand, sometimes the rational mean is not the real mean, but is considered in relation to us: and such is the mean in all the other moral virtues. The reason for this is that justice is about operations, which deal with external things, wherein the right has to be established simply and absolutely. Therefore the rational mean in justice gives to each one his due, neither more nor less. But the other moral virtues deal with interior passions, wherein the right cannot be established in the same way, since men are variously situated in relation to their passions; hence the rectitude of reason has to be established in the passions, with due regard to us, who are moved in respect to the passions" (I, II, 54, 2). "The other moral virtues are chiefly concerned with the passions, the regulation of which is gauged entirely by relation with the very man who is the subject of those passions, in so far as his anger and desire are vested

with their various due circumstances. Hence the mean in such virtues is measured not by the proportion of one thing to another, but merely by comparison with the virtuous man himself, so that with them the mean is only that which is fixed by reason with regard to ourselves" (II, II, 58, 10; cf. I, II, 60, 2; II, II, 61, 2 ad 1).

19 This is, of course, not intended to justify extreme subjectivism in personal decision, nor to deny the unconditional validity of general moral standards. Primarily, prudence means not leaving a decision to purely subjective feeling for values, but requiring the subject to act by the objective standard of reality. Furthermore, as we have noted, the essence of prudence is that it is directed toward the *means,* not toward the end; we have seen also that for prudence to act at all presupposes the dictates of the innate conscience (synderesis). Prudence includes synderesis. The innate conscience, however, is nothing else than the presence in the mind of the natural moral law; that is to say, speaking more specifically, of God's Ten Commandments. Therefore anything that contradicts the natural moral law can never—in *no* "concrete situation"—be prudent and good. Finally, as we have likewise indicated, the obligations of justice in the proper sense are to a particular degree independent of situation. Cf. in this connection what has been cited in connection with note 18.

The doctrine of prudence is no more and no less "subjectivistic" than the general Christian teaching that man is not allowed to act against his conscience (Rom. 14, 23), not even if this conscience be mistaken.

Above all, however, it is necessary to say that precisely the omission of special dictates for moral behavior distinguishes Christianity from Judaism, the period *post Christum natum* from the period *ante Christum natum.* Extreme casuistry has rightly been termed "Judaistic" (Linsenmann; cf. note 27) and "Talmudistic" (Hirscher; cf. note 27). The Law of the New Covenant is, as Thomas says in harmony with the Epistle of James (1, 25), "the law of perfect freedom"; "the Old Law, on the contrary, determined many things and left but little to be determined by human freedom" (I, II, 108, 1). "The New Law had no need to establish, by commandments and injunctions, any other external acts than the sacraments and the Commandments which in themselves belong to the essence of virtue, such as that we shall not kill, or steal, and other commandments of this sort" (I, II, 108, 2).

20 II, II, 47, 3.

21 Cf. note 15.

22 *"Prudentia plus importat quam scientia practica: nam ad scientiam practicam pertinet universale iudicium de agendis; sicut fornicationem esse malam, furtum non esse faciendum et huiusmodi. Qua quidem scientia existente, in particulari actu continget iudicium rationis intercipi, ut non recte diiudicet; et propter hoc dicitur parum valere ad virtutem, quia ea existente contingit hominem contra virtutem peccare. Sed ad prudentiam pertinet recte iudicare de singulis agibilibus, prout sint nunc agenda: quod quidem iudicium corrumpitur per quodlibet peccatum. Et ideo prudentia manente homo non peccat; unde ipsa non parum, sed multum confert ad virtutem; immo ipsam virtutem causat." Virt. comm.* 6 ad 1.

23 First, St. Thomas's concept of "art" does not mean primarily, as is the case today, the whole realm of artistic creation and of artistic products, but rather the inner attitude of the artist himself, by virtue of which he creates. Secondly, *ars* embraces both the realm of art proper and the realm of technical science. The shaping of an artifact according to certain "rules" is, to Thomas, the common element of art and technical science; there are no less plain standards for the "structure" of a sonnet and for the construction of a ship or a bridge. It is clear that the concept of *ars* in this sense is specifically medieval (and perhaps also specifically characteristic of Romance languages and thought). Cf. i. a. I, II, 57, 4.

24 *"Les manières d'être prudent, d'être moral, se renouvellent et se multiplient à l'infini, étant donnés l'instabilité et la variété des circonstances de la vie pratique; et pourtant, partout et toujours, nous sommes obligés d'être vertueux et de servir Dieu. La fin de l'art étant particulière et restreinte, l'artisan a, pour ainsi dire, la carte forcée dans le choix de ses moyens; du moins la variété de ces moyens n'est pas de rigueur; il suffit que ceux employés habituellement servent a réussir le type d'oeuvre que l'on a en vue. Il y a du procédé au fond de toute technique, et la science technique est précisément la science des meilleurs procédés. Il n'y a pas de procédés ne varietur en morale: la prudence vertueuse doit accomoder son discernement à l'instabilité des circonstances changeantes de la vie pratique. Pour autant qu'il tendrait à se fixer, le discernement se rapprocherait du procédé. La casuistique, poussée à l'excès, substitue des procédés et des recettes à l'infinie souplesse que doit garder la prudence vertueuse en face*

des complexités de la vie morale." H. D. Noble, O.P., in his above-mentioned commentary on the *Quaestiones on Prudence* in the French edition of the *Summa Theologica* (Paris, 1925), p. 238.

25 Paul Claudel, *L'Otage.*

26 *"Si la théologie morale était ramenée à la casuistique . . . elle deviendrait la science des péchés à éviter plutôt que celle des vertus à exercer et à parfaire."* Garrigou-Lagrange, "Du Caractère méta-physique de la théologie morale de Saint Thomas." *Revue thomiste,* vol. 8 (1925), p. 342.

27 Linsenmann, "Untersuchungen über die Lehre von Gesetz und Freiheit." *Theologische Quartalsschrift.* Tübingen, vol. 53 (1871), p. 238. "Entangled in such a Talmudistic spirit of pedantry, a man can scarcely take a step without his father confessor."—J. B. Hirscher, *Über das Verhältnis des Evangeliums zu der theologischen Scholastik der neuesten Zeit im katholischen Deutschland.* Tübingen, 1823, p. 238. In an outstanding treatise by P. Daniel Feuling, O.S.B., concerning prudence (which he denotes by an older word, *discretio*), he writes the following encouraging sentence: "Is there not among us a widespread tendency, though unconfessed, aimed at 'preserving' maturing and mature—perhaps we should do better to say, physically adult persons—as far as possible from making their own moral judg-ments and independent decisions of conscience? Are not general rules established (and we are not speaking here of their establish-ment and legislation by the proper authorities) concerning moral actions and moral life in the most diverse fields, rules which everyone is supposed to observe, rules which are intended to determine down to detail, and often down to triviality, what the moral order demands; rules which are then straightway equated with this moral order? And are we not at times inclined, and moreover quite ready, to raise the severe charge of immoral thinking and actions against those who balk at *such* casuistry and adhere to the great and fundamental moral truth that virtue lies in the mean, but not in an abstract, levelling mean, rather in the mean according to the circumstances, conditions, spiritual states, principles, and above all according to the person acting? It is really not surprising that given such tutelage and such influences, the indispensable practice in the virtue of distin-guishing and deciding according to circumstances, and therefore according to the real moral laws, is more or less omitted; and that,

moreover, virtually all moral courage to make independent moral decisions is undermined, and often lost entirely. In such a situation it is inevitable that many a less stanch soul grows despondent, confronts the moral life with helplessness and perplexity, and gives way to despair unless he finds a truly discreet person of firm judgment to give counsel and aid with his scruples. To combat these grave evils there is only *one* aid: persevering tutelage and training in *discretio.*" P. Daniel Feuling, O.S.B., "Discretio." *Benediktinische Monatsschrift,* vol. 7 (1925), pp. 359 f.

4. PRUDENCE AND CHARITY

1 *Ver.* 14, 6.

2 II, II, 47, 13 ad 2.

3 I, II, 18, 5.

4 Cf. *Die Wirklichkeit und das Gute,* pp. 52 ff., on the structure of moral "total action."

5 *"Prudentia praecise dirigit in his quae sunt ad finem. . . . Sed finis agibilium praexistit in nobis dupliciter: scil. per cognitionem naturalem de fine hominis [synderesis!]; alio modo quantum ad affectionem: et sic fines agibilium sunt in nobis per virtutes morales. . . . Ad prudentiam requiruntur et intellectus finium et virtutes morales, quibus affectus recte collocatur in fine; et propter hoc oportet omnem prudentem virtuosum esse." Ver.* 5, 1.

6 "How this inner penetration of practical cognition and its reflection, judging and deciding [by the will; J.P.], takes place, is a question that touches upon mysteries. But this mystery is experienced reality and the condition of all morality, and we may well say that in its character of a mystery, light is cast upon it by the metaphysical nature of the mind. For as cognition the mind is directed toward all being, including action and its moral determinants; and as will the mind is directed toward all good, including the goodness of cognition, especially that aspect of cognition which is of practical importance. This directing springs from the ultimate depths of the mind's being and nature." P. Daniel Feuling, O.S.B., "Discretio." *Benediktinische Monatsschrift,* vol. 7 (1925), p. 256.

7 *"Ad actum virtutis requiritur, quod sit rectus et quod sit voluntarius. Sed sicut voluntarii actus principium est voluntas, ita recti actus principium est ratio." Ver.* 14, 5, obj. 11.

8 Cf. *Die Wirklichkeit und das Gute*, p. 109.
9 *Virt. card.* 2.
10 *Ver.* 27, 5 ad 5.
11 *Ver.* 14, 5 ad 11.
12 II, II, 52, 2.
13 II, II, 52, 2 ad 3.
14 II, II, 52, 2 ad 1.
15 I, II, 61, 5.

JUSTICE

1. ON RIGHTS

1 Kant, *Eine Vorlesung über Ethik*, Paul Menzer (2d edition, Berlin 1925), p. 245.
2 Thomas Aquinas, *In Eth.*, 5, 1; No. 893.
3 *Republic* 331.—Plato quotes the poet Simonides who lived over a century earlier than he did. Simonides, however, is not the author of this idea, for it is formulated already in Homer, in the *Odyssey* (14, 84).
4 *Rhetoric* 1, 9.
5 *De finibus* 5, 23.
6 *De officiis* 1, 24.
7 *The City of God* 19, 21.
8 *Corpus Juris Civilis, Instit.* I, 1.
9 II, II, 58, 1.—It is a matter, as Thomas says, of repeating, in the proper form of a definition, the formula encountered in Roman Law.
10 *Virt. Card.*, I ad 12.
11 *In Div. Nom.*, 8, 4; No. 778.
12 *Patrologia Latina* (Migne), 220, 633.
13 *C.G.* 2, 28.
14 *Ibid.*
15 *Ibid.*
16 *Non igitur creatio ex debito justitiae procedit. C.G.* 2, 28.
17 I, 21, 1 ad 3.
18 II, II, 57, 1.
19 Thomas says in the *Summa Contra Gentes* (2, 93): *Quod ad perfectionem alicujus requiritur* belongs to man, and therefore, those

things that a man necessarily has. Need and necessity (*exigentia, necessitas*) are expressed in "belonging to" (I, 21, 1 ad 3). In the once famous book by R. von Ihering, *Der Zweck im Recht*, it is stated: "To have a right means: There is something there for us" Volksausgabe I, p. 49. Emil Brunner (*Gerechtigkeit*, Zurich 1943) speaks of the "order of rights" into which man finds himself introduced by the idea of justice (p. 22).

20 Plato, *Gorgias* 469.

21 *Ibid.* 508.

22 II, II, 57, 2.

23 II, II, 57, 2 ad 2.

24 We can, of course, in a very improper sense, speak of a person treating an animal "justly" or "unjustly"; we can even say that cruelty to animals is "unjust." Something of the same sort occurs in the usual expression of the "material justice" of an artistic action. In the exact meaning of the word, however, beings that are not spiritual do not have inalienable rights; something cannot properly "belong" to them; they themselves, rather, belong to man.

25 J. Leclerq, "Note sur la justice," *Revue Néoscolastique de Philosophie*, 28th year (1926), p. 269.

26 J.-P. Sartre, *Existentialism*, Philosophical Library (New York 1947) p. 18.

27 *C.G.* 3, 112.

28 *C.G.* 3, 112.

29 *Vorlesung über Ethik*, p. 245.

30 4 d. 26, 1, 2, 1.

31 Cf. Josef Pieper, *Traktat über die Klugheit* (4th ed., Munich 1950), especially the second chapter "Knowledge of the reality and realization of the good." *(Das Wissen um die Wirklichkeit und die Verwirklichung des Guten.)*

2. DUTY IN RELATION TO "THE OTHER"

1 II, 57, 1.

2 Thomas speaks of *alietas* and *diversitas*: II, II, 58, 2.

3 Of course, there is also a broader notion of justice that does not exclude charity, just as there is also a notion of charity that includes within itself the notion of justice.

4 II, II, 58, 2.

5 II, II, 57, 4.

6 In Franz Dornseiff, *Der deutsche Wortschatz* (3rd ed., Berlin 1943) the word *"Ohrenbläserei"* (tale bearing) is assigned to the word-group "flattery" (p. 556).

7 II, II, 74, 2.

8 *Justitia consistit in communicatione. In Eth.* 8, 9; No. 1658.

9 II, II, 102, 2 ad 2.

10 *Dependet ex honestate debentia.* II, II, 106, 4 ad 1.

11 *Inter virtutes morales sola justitia potest Deo magis proprie attribui. In Div. Nom.,* 8, 4; No. 771.

12 I, 21, 4.

13 *Reddit sibi quod sibi debetur.* I, 21, 1 ad 3.

14 *Proslogion* 10.

15 I, 21, 1 ad 3.

16 *Alteri obligatum esse.* II, II, 122, 1.

17 *Republic* 332.

18 II, II, 122, 1.

19 II, II, 122, 1.

20 II, II, 122, 1, *sed contra.*

21 II, II, 58, 5.

22 Thomas interprets (II, II, 58, 5 ad 3) the text from the New Testament (I John 3, 4) in the following sense—every sin is *in-iquitas.*

23 *Virt. card.* 3 ad 8; II, II, 58, 6 ad 4; 79, 1.

24 II, II, 47, 10 ad 1; *In Eth.* 5, 2; No. 907.

25 II, II, 58, 5.

26 *In Eth.* 5, 2; No. 907.

27 *Nichomach. Ethics* 5, 3; 1129b.

28 II, II, 79, 1.

29 *In Eth.* 5, 1; No. 886.

30 *Lecture on Ethics,* p. 245.

31 I, II, 100, 2.

32 *Secundum rationem commensurationis ad alterum.* I, II, 60, 2.

33 3 d. 33, 2, 1, 3.

34 I, II, 60, 2.

35 Cf. Joseph Pieper, *Fortitude and Temperance* (Pantheon, New York 1954) pp. 61 ff.

36 Commentary on I, II, 60, 2.

37 *Virt. card.* I ad 12.

38 II, II, 122, 1.

39 II, II, 181, 1 ad 1.

40 I, II, 100, 9 ad 1.—It should not go unsaid that this statement is made with regard to the law of the *Old* Covenant. Yet the text that has been quoted is not immediately affected by this restriction.

41 This example is cited by Sertillanges in his *Philosophie Morale de S. Thomas* (Paris 1922), p. 244.

42 *In Eth.* 5, 13; No. 1044.

43 5, 9 f.

44 I, II, 107, 4.—This statement, once again by way of merely noting the point, was made in a question about the law of the *New* Covenant.

45 II, II, 58, 10.

3. THE RANK OF JUSTICE

1 *De officiis* 1, 7.

2 II, II, 58, 3.

3 Thus writes Ambrose in his *De officiis* (1, 35), a book that is also inspired by Cicero's writing of the same title.

4 *C.G.* 3, 24.

5 *In Eth.* 5, 2; No. 910.

6 I, II, 66, 4.

7 II, II, 58, 12; I, II, 66, 1.

8 *Virt. commun.* 9.

9 I, II, 66, 4.

10 II, II, 124, 1.

11 *Justitia est hujus boni factiva.* II, II, 123, 12.

12 II, II, 157, 4.

13 II, II, 123, 12.

14 II, II, 123, 12.

15 *Per eam (=justitiam) applicatur voluntas ad proprium actum.* I, II, 59, 5.

16 *In Eth.* 5, 15; No. 1077.

17 Plontinus, *Enneads* I, 2, 6: Διχαιοσυνη δε ειπεϱ διχειοπϱαγια.

18 II, II, 55, 8.

19 Cf. Josef Pieper, *The End of Time* (Pantheon, New York 1954), the chapter about the figure of Antichrist.

4. THE THREE BASIC FORMS OF JUSTICE

1 Diogenes Laertius, *Lives and Opinions* I, 36.
2 Plutarch, *Banquet of the Seven Wise Men*, ch. 11.
3 *Reg. princ.* 1, 10.
4 The text is handed on in Aristotle's *Nichomachean Ethics* (5, 3; 1130a).
5 Plutarch, *Banquet*, ch. 11.
6 *Ibid.*
7 Diogenes Laertius, *Lives and Opinions* I, 69.
8 Plutarch, *Banquet*, ch. 11.
9 *Ibid.*
10 II, II, 61, 1.
11 *In Eth.* 1, 1; No. 5.
12 Cf. in addition O. Spann, *Gesellschaftslehre* (3rd ed., Leipzig 1930) p. 157 f.

5. RECOMPENSE AND RESTITUTION

1 I, II, 114, 1.–*Simpliciter . . . justum est inter aequales.* III, 85, 3.
2 4 d. 46, 1, 1, 1.–cf. *C.G.* 1, 93; 1, 21, 1; *In Div. Nom.* 8, 4; No. 775.
3 *Commutationes, secundum quas transfertur aliquid ab uno in alterum. . . . In Eth.* 5, 4; No. 928.
4 II, II, 61, 3.
5 Cf. Josef Pieper, *Grundformen sozialer Spielregeln* (2nd ed., Frankfurt 1950), particularly the chapter "Die Spielregeln der Gesellschaft."
6 II, II, 62, 1.
7 This is the translation of M. S. Gillet, O.P., in the French-Latin *Summa Theologica* in the Editions de la Revue des Jeunes (Paris-Tournai-Rome 1932); II, II, 61 proœmium.
8 II, II, 62, 1.
9 So, for example, B. H. Merkelbach, *Summa Theologiae Moralis* (2nd ed., Paris 1936), II, 284.
10 *Grundlagen der Moral.* Collected Works (Insel ed.), II, p. 611.
11 II, II, 61, 3.
12 II, II, 61, 3.
13 *Per restitutionem fit reductio ad aequalitatem.* II, II, 62, 5.

6. DISTRIBUTIVE JUSTICE

1 II, II, 58, 7 ad 2.

2 II, II, 61, 1 ad 5.

3 II, II, 61, 2.

4 I, 21, 1; cf. also *In Eth.* 5, 4; No. 927, 928.

5 II, II, 61, 2.

6 II, II, 61, 2.

7 II, II, 61, 2 ad 2.

8 *In Eth.* 5, 6; No. 950.

9 *Nichomach. Ethics* 5, 7; 1131b.

10 *In Pol.* 1, 1; No. 11.

11 The idea of "mutilation" is not as "medieval" as it may first appear. Sterilization as a measure of punishment exists, for instance, in modern states; and in the right to it, as a matter of principle, is not denied even by the Church. Cf., for example, *Lexicon für Theologie und Kirche*, vol. 9, col. 813.

12 II, II, 65, 2 ad 2.

13 *In Eth.* 5, 11; No. 1009.

14 *In Ephes.* 6, 3.

15 This apparently is not true of the West's classical doctrine of justice alone. For Chung-Sho Lo, a professor of philosophy and Chinese member of the Unesco Commission that has prepared the new formulation of human rights, made the point, much to people's embarrassment, that in the Chinese tradition there is no concept of human right and the Chinese language does not possess any word exactly corresponding to our word "right." There is, of course, a notion of "justice" and also a much different doctrine of the justice of the sovereign. To this effect Chung-Sho Lo quoted the *Book of Stories*, a book almost two thousand years old: "Heaven loves the people and the sovereign must obey heaven." Cf. *Um die Erklärung der Menschenrechte* (Zurich 1951), p. 242 ff.

16 Cf. also on this point Romano Guardini, *Die Macht* (Würzburg 1951) p. 91 f.

17 "There will be no longer any proper political power," says K. Marx (*Elend der Philosophie*, Berlin 1952, p. 194).

18 *Pol.* 3, 4; 1276b.

19 On this score Thomas says that in the best state it is not pos-

sible to be a good citizen without that capacity in virtue of which a man is a good man. *In Pol.* 3, 3; No. 366; cf. *In Eth.* 5, 3; No. 926.

20 Thomas quotes him as follows: *"Principatus virum ostendit." Reg. princ.* 1, 10.

21 *Reg. princ.* 1, 8.

22 The Commentary on the *Nichomachean Ethics* says, honor and glory are the best things that men may give to the just ruler; naturally, the tyrant wants material gain over and above that. *In Eth.* 5, 11; No. 1011.

23 *Reg. princ.* 1, 10.

24 *Divine Comedy*, Paradiso, canto 18.

25 *Pol.* 3, 4; 1277b.

26 II, II, 50, 1 ad 1.

27 *Reg. princ.* 1, 4.

28 *Reg. princ.* 1, 6.

29 "The proletarian state is a machine for the suppression of the bourgeoisie"; "dictatorship of the proletariat is the government of the proletariat over the bourgeoisie, a government that is restricted by no law and that rests on power." J. Stalin, *Uber die Grundlagen des Leninismus* (Berlin 1946), p. 30 f.

30 It concerned the iron dispute of the Northwest group and Wissell, the federal minister of labor at that time.

31 Conditions in England, for instance, are undoubtedly different from those in Germany. Yet in this field no settlement is valid once and for all. We must, however, see the point political self-discipline must attain, if a serious settlement is to come into effect.

32 II, II, 61, 1 ad 3.

33 I, II, 96, 6.

34 Donoso Cortes, *Der Abfall vom Abendland*. Dokumente. Published by Paul Viator (Vienna 1948), p. 67.

35 II, II, 61, 2.

36 The next paragraph is a self-quotation from Josef Pieper, *Thesen zur sozialen Politik* (Freiburg 1946), p. 8.

37 Encyclical *Quadragesimo anno*.

38 4 d. 26, 1, 2.

39 *Opponitur justitiae distributivae.* II, II, 63, prologue.

40 II, II, 63.

41 II, II, 63, 2.

42 II, II, 63, 1.

43 II, II, 63, 1.

44 II, II, 63, 2.

45 Aelred of Rievaux, *On Spiritual Friendship*, III, 4 (PL. 195, 697-698).

46 *Laws* 757.

7. THE LIMITS OF JUSTICE

1 II, II, 80, 1.

2 I, 21, 1 ad 3.

3 I, 21, 4.

4 II, II, 85, 1.—*All* men, the *Summa Theologica* goes on to say (II, II, 86, 4 ad 2), knew at least implicitly the meaning of sacrifice.

5 *Gorgias* 480.

6 III, 85, 3 ad 2.

7 II, II, 80, 1.

8 II, II, 101, 1.

9 *Personae in dignitate constitutae* (II, II, 102, 1); *personae dignitate praecellentes* II, II, 103, 3).

10 II, II, 80, 1.

11 In an enumeration that is not intended to be complete, Thomas speaks (II, II, 102, 1) of sovereigns, generals, masters: *et simile est in aliis.*

12 II, II, 103, 2 ad 2.

13 Emil Brunner (*Gerechtigkeit,* p. 50) refers to Rousseau on this score. He (Rousseau) would have the family dissolve itself as soon as cooperation is no longer necessary, so that the children might attain full independence as quickly as possible, that alone being suitable for men.

14 II, II, 106, 4.

15. II, II, 114, 2 ad 1.

16 It is scarcely necessary to go into any details concerning the appalling timeliness of this idea. In a report on his imprisonment (. . . *Und führen wohin Du nicht willst,* 4th ed., Munich 1952; English tr. *Unwilling Journey,* Muhlenberg Press, Philadelphia) H. Gollwitzer, speaking of his own experience, said that "old prisoners" would only let their comrades, who had perhaps become ill, share in their allotted ration in accordance with the output they actually achieved: "They could as little understand our appeal to sympathy

and comradeship as we could understand their stubborn calculation of what belonged to each man—a calculation on which the Soviet Union's whole system of living is erected" (p. 101).

17 *In Matth.* 5, 2.
18 *C.G.* 3, 130.

FORTITUDE

1. READINESS TO FALL IN BATTLE

1 *Quol.* 4, 20.
2 *Martyrdom of St. Polycarp,* 4.
3 *The Proconsular Acts of St. Cyprian,* 1.
4 II, II, 123, 8.
5 *Serm.* 16; quoted in II, II, 124, 4, sed contra.
6 Tertullian, *Apologeticum,* 50.
7 II, II, 123, 8.

2. FORTITUDE MUST NOT TRUST ITSELF

1 II, II, 125, 2 ad 2.
2 *Virt. card.* 4 ad 5.
3 II, II, 124, 3.
4 II, II, 123, 12 ad 2.
5 *De officiis* 1, 35.
6 II, II, 129, 5 ad 2.
7 II, II, 126, 2 ad 1.
8 Thucydides, *Peloponnesian War,* Book II.
9 II, II, 123, 12.
10 *Enarrationes in Psalmos* 34, 13.
11 II, II, 123, 12 ad 3.
12 *De officiis* I, 35.

3. ENDURANCE AND ATTACK

1 II, II, 123, 1 ad 2.
2 II, II, 123, 4.
3 II, II, 123, 6.

4 II, II, 123, 6 ad 2.
5 II, II, 136, 4 ad 2.
6 I, II, 66, 4 ad 2; II, II, 128, 1.
7 II, II, 128, 1.
8 Scivias III, 22.
9 II, II, 136, 2 ad 2.
10 I, II, 66, 4 ad 2; *Virt. card.* 1 ad 4.
11 II, II, 128, 1 ad 2.
12 II, II, 123, 10 ad 3.
13 St. Athanasius, *Third Oration against the Arians,* chap. 57.
14 *In John* 18, lect. 4, 2.

4. VITAL, MORAL, MYSTIC FORTITUDE

1 Fritz Künkel, *Neurasthenie und Hysterie; Handbuch der Individualpsychologie* (ed. E. Wexberg; Munich, 1926) p. 500.
2 I, II, 68, 2.
3 I, II, 62, 5.
4 I, II, 62, 5.
5 II, II, 159, 2 ad 1.
6 St. Teresa of Avila, *Autobiography,* chap. 31, 18.
7 II, II, 139, 1.

TEMPERANCE

2. SELFLESS SELF-PRESERVATION

1 4, d. 14, 1, 1, 4 ad 2; II, II, 141, 2 obj. 2.
2 II, II, 141, 8.
3 *Virt. card.* 4; I, II, 61, 5.
4 II, II, 141, 2 ad 2.
5 I, 60, 5.
6 II, II, 23, 7.
7 E. Przywara, *Das Geheimnis Kierkegaards,* Munich, 1929, p. 77 f.
8 II, II, 141, 4.
9 II, II, 161; 162.
10 II, II, 157; 158.
11 II, II, 166; 167.

3. CHASTITY AND UNCHASTITY

1 *Mal.* 15, 2.

2 "As the use of foods can be without sin, if it be done in a proper manner and order, according to what befits bodily health: thus also the use of sex can be without any sin, if it be done in a proper manner and order, according to what is suitable to the purpose of human propagation." II, II, 153, 2.

3 *Ibid.*

4 II, II, 142, 1; 152, 2 ad 2; 153, 3 ad 3.

5 4, d. 33, 1, 1.

6 *Twelfth Homily on the Epistle to the Colossians.* I owe this quotation to the excellent book of August Adam, *Der Primat der Liebe*, Kevelaer, no date.

7 II, II, 153,

8 II, II, 151, 1.

9 II, II, 153, 3; 154, 1.

10 Cf. Josef Pieper, *Die Wirklichkeit und das Gute*, Leipzig, 1935. p. 84 f.

11 II, II, 153, 3 ad 2.

12 Cf. also II, II, 152, 2; 146, 1 ad 1.

13 II, II, 151, 4.

14 I, II, 18, 5.

15 II, II, 153, obj. 2, ad 2.

16 I, 98, 2.

17 I, 98, 2 ad 3.

18 II, II, 154, 1 ad 2.

19 II, II, 153, 3; *Mal.* 15, 2 ad 4.

20 II, II, 122, 1; 122, 6.

21 II, II, 153, 5 ad 1.

22 *Ibid.*

23 II, II, 15, 3.

24 II, II, 53, 6 ad 2.

25 II, II, 180, 2 ad 3.

26 II, II, 155, 1 ad 2.

27 *Enarrationes in psalmos* 72, 32.

28 *Mal.* 15, 4: (*ratio*), *secundum quod dirigit humanos actus:* (reason), in accordance with the fact that it directs human actions.

29 II, II, 153, 5 ad 1.
30 Cf. *Die Wirklichkeit und das Gute,* p. 53ff.
31 *Mal.* 15, 4.
32 II, II, 155, 4; 156, 3.
33 II, II, 155, 4 ad 3.
34 II, II, 155, 4; *Virt. card.* 1 ad 6; II, II, 123, 12 ad 2.
35 *Nicomachean Ethics,* 7, 9 (^{1}151a).
36 II, II, 156, 3 ad 1.
37 II, II, 156, 3.
38 *Ibid.*
39 *Mal.* 3, 13.
40 *Ibid.*
41 Cf. Aristotle, *Nicomachean Ethics, loc. cit.*
42 I, II, 64, 2.
43 *Somme théologique* La tempérance, tome 2, Paris, 1928, p. 324.
44 II, II, 170, 1 ad 3.
45 *Quol.* 12, 33.
46 II, II, 154, 4; *Ver.* 15, 4.
47 I cannot recall having run across the expression *partes in-honestae* (indecent parts) anywhere in the writings of St. Thomas. Yet this expression, very suspicious in itself, might have some meaning in regard to man, if used with the necessary reservations (cf. Lactantius, *De opificio Dei,* 13); namely that the constant possibility of a rebellion of the senses against the spirit becomes most likely and most obvious in the generative organs (II, II, 154, 4). But the expression becomes completely meaningless when referring to an animal. It may also be noted that such a book as the *Vademecum theologiae moralis* (Handbook of Moral Theology) by Fr. Prümmer, O.Praem. (Freiburg, 1921), which despite its usually strong reliance on the structure of the second part of the *Summa Theologica,* likewise contains chapters entitled "Touch," "Glances," etc., yet is silent on the subject here mentioned, whereas it says, concerning the *tactus inhonestus bestiarum* (indecent touching of animals): "It must be judged according to the intention and condition of the person touching" (p. 291).
48 II, II, 141, 4 ad 3; cf. also *Mal.* 8, 1 ad 9.
49 I, 5, 4 ad 1.

50 *Ratio imitatur naturam* (reason imitates nature) I, 60, 5. "Since those things which are according to nature, have been ordered by Divine reason, which human reason ought to imitate, whatever is done according to human reason which is against the order commonly found in natural things, is defective (*vitiosum*) and a sin." II, II, 130, 1. Cf. also II, II, 133, 1; Car. 1.

51 *In II Cor. 4, 5;* cf. *In Rom.* 7, 4; *C.G.* 1, 20.

52 *De oratione* 22.

53 *De pudicitia* 1.

54 *De spectaculis* 24.

55 II, II, 8, 7.

56 The passage runs as follows: "Be strict, then, in taking them to task, so that they may be soundly established in the faith, instead of paying attention to these Jewish fables, these rules laid down for them by human teachers who will not look steadily at the truth. As if anything could be unclean for those who have clean hearts! But for these men, defiled as they are by want of faith, everything is unclean; defilement has entered their very thought, their very consciences. They profess recognition of God, but their practice contradicts it. . ." Titus I: 13–16.

57 II, II, 142, 2 ad 2; 142, 3.

58 II, II, 141, 8 ad 3.

59 *Omne peccatum formaliter consistit in aversione a Deo* (Every sin consists formally in a turn away from God). II, II, 10, 3; 148, 5 ad 2.

60 Adam, *op. cit.,* p. 110.

61 II, II, 20, 3.

62 II, II, 154, 3 ad 1.

63 Cf. Adam, *op. cit.,* p. 210.

64 II, II, 154, 3 ad 1 (cf. also the objection that goes with this); II, II, 150, 3 ad 1.

65 II, II, 123, 12.

66 II, II, 141, 8.

67 It is only the theological virtues, prudence and justice, says St. Thomas, that "simply" direct man toward the good. II, II, 157, 4.

4. VIRGINITY

1 II, II, 152, 3; 152, 3 ad 5.

2 St. Augustine, *De virginitate* 8.

3 II, II, 152, 3; 152, 3 ad 1; 152, 5.

4 ". . . that, whereas no forbiddance has diminished the honorable state of marriage and the nuptial benediction abides upon Holy Matrimony, there might nonetheless exist more exalted souls, who would disdain the married state as far as the physical union of man and wife is concerned, yet desire the sacrament, nor would imitate what is done in marriage, but would love that which is designated for marriage." *Pontificale Romanum, De benedictione et consecratione virginum* (On the Blessing and Consecration of Virgins).

5 Quoted in an essay by Maria Schlüter-Hermkes on St. Catherine of Genoa in *Die Christliche Frau,* 1924.

6 The title of the first chapter of the *De perfectione vitae spiritualis* reads: "That the perfection of spiritual life is attained simply according to the love of God."

7 *De bono conjugali* 22.

8 *De virginitate* 44.

9 II, II, 152, 2, obj. 1; 152, 4, obj. 2.

10 II, II, 152, 2 ad 1.

11 II, II, 152, 4.

5. ON FASTING

1 II, II, 146, 1 ad 4.

2 *Quaestiones evangeliorum;* quoted in II, II, 146, 1 ad 2.

3 II, II, 147, 3.

4 *Ibid.*

5 II, II, 146, 1 ad 4.

6. *Quol.* 5, 18.

7 II, II, 146, 1 ad 2.

8 II, II, 147, 1 ad 2.

9 "In such a way, however, that thereby nature is not grievously burdened." II, II, 147, 7; cf. II, II, 147, 6.

10 II, II, 147, 5 ad 3.

11 II, II, 150, 1 ad 1.
12 *Quol.* 5, 18.
13 II, II, 148, 6; *Mal.* 14, 4.
14 *Divine Comedy*, Purgatory XXIII, 31ff; Norton translation.
15 *Regula pastoralis* 3, 19.

6. THE SENSE OF TOUCH

1 II, II, 141, 4.
2 *Ibid.* It should be noted here that St. Thomas does not think that the sense of taste is only a special form of the sense of touch; cf. *Mal.* 14, 3 ad 4.
3 *Ver.* 22, 5.
4 I, 76, 5.
5 *In An.* 8.
6 *Ibid.*
7 *In An.* 3, 18.
8 I, 76, 5.
9 *In An.* 2, 19.
10 I, 76, 5.
11 *In An.* 2, 19; cf. *An.* 8.
12 III, 15, 6; 26, 3 ad 9.
13 *Blätter und Steine,* Hamburg, 1934, p. 171f.
14 II, II, 141, 6 ad 1.

7. HUMILITY

1 *Mal.* 8, 2. "From all our goods we seek some excellence." I, II, 47, 2.
2 II, II, 161, 6; 162, 3 ad 2.
3 II, II, 161, 1 ad 3; 129, 3 ad 4.
4 II, II, 162, 1 ad 3.
5 II, II, 129, 1.
6 II, II, 129, 3 ad 5.
7 II, II, 129, 2.
8 II, II, 129, 1 ad 3.
9 II, II, 129, 2 ad 3.
10 II, II, 129, 3 ad 4.
11 *Ibid.*

12 II, II, 129, 4 ad 2.
13 II, II, 129, 3 ad 5.
14 II, II, 129, 4 ad 2.
15 II, II, 129, 6.
16 II, II, 129, 7.
17 II, II, 129, 7 sed contra.
18 Johannes Cassianus, *De coenob. instit.* 12, 7.
19 II, II, 162, 5; 161, 1 ad 5; 161, 2 ad 3; 161, 6.
20 II, II, 161, 3 ad 3.
21 II, II, 161, 3.
22 Cf. Brother Leo, *Mirror of Perfection,* chap. LXI.
23 *Epist. ad Januarium* 54, 4.

8. THE POWER OF WRATH

1 I, II, 23, 1 ad 1.
2 *Ad invadendum malum laesivum.* I, II, 23, 3.
3 I, 81, 2.
4 *Mal.* 12, 1.
5 II, II, 158, 1.
6 "To act from passion diminishes both honor and reproach, but to act *with* passion can increase both." *Ver.* 26, 7 ad 1.
7 *Moralia* in Job 5: 45.
8 II, II, 158, 1 ad 2; cf. *Mal.* 12, 1 ad 4.
9 II, II, 158, 5.
10 II, II, 157, 4 ad 1.
11 *Tumor mentis. Mal.* 12, 5.
12 II, II, 157, 1.
13 II, II, 157, 4.
14 II, II, 158, 8; *Mal.* 12, 5 ad 3.
15 II, II, 156, 4.
16 II, II, 158, 4.
17 II, II, 35, 1 ad 4.
18 *Ver.* 24, 10.

9. DISCIPLINING THE EYES

1 *Confessions* 10, 35.
2 II, II, 166, 2 ad 3.

3 II, II, 167, 1 ad 3.
4 *Sprüche in Prosa.*
5 II, II, 167, 1.
6 *Confessions* 10, 35.
7 *De vera religione* 53.
8 2nd ed., Halle, 1929, p. 172.
9 Cf. Josef Pieper, *Über die Hoffnung,* 2nd ed., Leipzig, 1938, p. 55 ff.
10 *Mal.* 11, 4.
11 II, II,35, 3 ad 3.
12 *Sein und Zeit,* p. 173.

10. THE FRUITS OF TEMPERANCE

1 II, II, 142, 4.
2 II, II, 153, 5 ad 2.
3 II, II, 142, 2.
4 II, II, 142, 4; 151, 4 ad 2.
5 II, II, 153, 5 ad 2. St. Thomas here quotes Scripture: "Dalliance and wine and revelry . . . steal·away your wits." Osee 4: 11.
6 Dogmatic decision of the Council of Vienne (1311 to 1312); cf. Denziger, *Enchiridion symbolorum,* 481.
7 II, II, 161, 6 ad 2.
8 Cf. Josef Pieper, *Über die Hoffnung,* p. 49ff.
9 Cf. also *Mal.* 15, 4 ad 3; II, II, 153, 4 ad 2.
10 *Collationes patrum* 1, 4.
11 *De moribus Ecclesiae* 15.
12 *Poetics* 6, 2 (1449b).
13 II, II, 141, 1 ad 3.

312-924-1000

Tichtmob 31   831-1

10:us-

Tichtmote   312-559-1240

9-